Managing Your TIAA-CREF Retirement Accounts

Investment Strategies to Maximize Retirement Income

Leonard E. Goodall
Professor of Management and Public Administration
University of Nevada, Las Vegas

William J. Corney
Professor of Management
University of Nevada, Las Vegas

KENDALL/HUNT PUBLISHING COMPANY
2460 Kerper Boulevard   P.O. Box 539   Dubuque, Iowa 52004-0539

Copyright © 1990 by Kendall/Hunt Publishing Company

Library of Congress Catalog Card Number: 89-63592

ISBN 0-8403-5631-5

All rights reserved. No part of this publication may be reproduced, stored in a retrieval system, or transmitted, in any form or by any means, electronic, mechanical, photocopying, recording, or otherwise, without the prior written permission of the copyright owner.

Printed in the United States of America
10 9 8 7 6 5 4 3 2 1

Contents

v	Introduction	
1	Chapter 1	Financial Planning and Retirement Planning
11	Chapter 2	TIAA-CREF and Other Options
19	Chapter 3	Choosing an Investment Strategy
29	Chapter 4	Asset Allocation Strategies
41	Chapter 5	Dollar Averaging Strategies
47	Chapter 6	Transferring Accumulations
77	Chapter 7	The New TIAA-CREF Offerings
93	Chapter 8	Using TIAA-CREF Services
109	Chapter 9	Your Other Investments
135	Selected Readings	
139	Appendix A	Selected TIAA-CREF Publications
140	Appendix B	TIAA-CREF Toll-free Numbers
141	Appendix C	Some Independent Companies Offering Tax Sheltered Annuities
142	Appendix D	Investment Software Programs
146	Appendix E	Useful Addresses
151	Index	

Introduction

Retirement planning has undergone dramatic changes in recent years. Longer life spans, changing mandatory retirement laws, and early retirement incentive programs are only a few examples of this trend. In higher education, in particular, the changes have been far reaching, and they are still occurring.

TIAA-CREF, the primary retirement organization for universities and many other non-profit associations, is in the process of policy changes that will give the individual participant much more flexibility but at the cost of increased responsibility. Those changes are the subject of this book.

Most university faculty and staff who were participants in TIAA-CREF in the past gave little thought to retirement planning. When they filled out their employment forms, they probably divided their retirement contributions between TIAA and CREF with little thought (many just put 50% in each), and then forgot about it. Some participants may still choose to do that, but the cost of doing so will be much higher in the future. TIAA-CREF is in the process of providing several additional investment options which will offer different kinds of investment opportunities and different levels of risk.

This book offers investment strategies that we hope will be of use to readers with little knowledge of or interest in investing as well as to readers with a desire to commit considerable amounts of time to enhancing their retirement income. The reader with some knowledge of computers will find suggestions for investment strategies which can be implemented through spending a few minutes each week using the computer for data input and analysis.

The strategies discussed are based on TIAA-CREF's planned investment options, but we would point out that they can be used with options offered by other investment companies as well. Many institutions today provide employees a choice among TIAA-CREF and other retirement plans. Our strategies should be useful regardless of which investment organization holds your retirement funds.

We need to emphasize, here and throughout the book, that TIAA-CREF has not yet implemented all of the investment options which it has in the planning stages. They have plans for as many as eight options, including a bond fund, an international stock fund, other new stock funds, and a revised TIAA which will permit transfers of funds out as well as in. Some of the strategies we discuss assume the availability of all of these. As you consider using a particular strategy, you will need to check with TIAA-CREF to see whether the new options in which you are interested have been implemented. Most of the plans we describe can be used even if only a few of the new options have been made available.

This book has been written independently of TIAA-CREF. We have no connection with the organization other than participating in their retirement plans through our employer, the University of Nevada, Las Vegas. The book is in no way a publication of that organization, and they were not aware of its contents prior to publication.

We do, however, want to thank TIAA-CREF for their cooperation and help in the preparation of the book. They provided historical data and other information to us which was of great assistance. In particular, we express appreciation to Dr. Francis P. King, Senior Research Officer, for his willingness to respond to our requests for information. In addition, Dr. Robert H. Atwell, President of the American Council on Education and a Trustee of TIAA Stock and Member of CREF, gave early encouragement to us to proceed with the project.

The content of the book, both facts and recommendations, is solely our responsibility. We hope you, the reader, find it both interesting and useful.

> Leonard E. Goodall
> Professor of Management
> and Public Administration
> University of Nevada, Las Vegas
>
> William J. Corney
> Professor of Management
> University of Nevada, Las Vegas
>
> November, 1989

Chapter 1

Financial Planning and Retirement Planning

You are probably a bit unhappy about having to read this book in the first place. You never really wanted to manage your own retirement funds. You thought your employer or a professional pension fund manager was taking care of that. Now you have discovered that, because you are offered so many investment options, your retirement income may be greatly affected by decisions you make (or don't make!).

It is likely that your interest in money management is limited. If that were your interest, you would have become a banker or stockbroker. Instead you became a professor of history, English or engineering. Or perhaps you are a university registrar, librarian, admissions officer or even a football coach. In any case your priorities call for you to spend most of your time on matters other than money management. If you see yourself in the above comments, this book is written especially for you.

If you are a professor of finance, investments or financial planning, it is possible this book is not for you. You may already have more knowledge than you will find here. Even you, however, may want to review some of the technical and computer-aided strategies outlined here to see if they can be of use to you.

However much or little interest you may have in financial matters, there is a saying on Wall Street which you should keep in mind—NO ONE ELSE IS AS INTERESTED IN YOUR MONEY AS YOU ARE. Your attorney, accountant, financial planner, broker, next door neighbor or cocktail party companion will all be willing to give you advice. Remember, though, that as interested as investment professionals may be in helping you, they are also interested in their own service charges, commissions, brokerage fees, etc. The overwhelming majority of such people are honest and competent, but they are also human beings. If you totally abdicate all management of your financial affairs and turn it entirely over to them, you will probably pay a price for that action. The price will not be just in fees or commissions you pay but also in the fact that no one else will share your intense interest and concern about your financial resources.

This book is primarily about retirement planning, especially for those whose retirement funds are invested through Teachers Insurance and Annuity-College Retirement Equities Fund (TIAA-CREF). The investment principles outlined here, however, will apply equally well to retirement funds offered by other investment companies.

Retirement planning, of course, is only one aspect of a total approach to personal financial planning. This is not the place for a full-scale discussion of personal financial planning, but you may want to refer to some of the books on that subject which are listed in the bibliography. We will discuss financial planning here in just enough detail to explain where retirement planning fits into your total personal financial planning picture.

Personal Financial Planning

Personal financial planning, like most any planning effort, is a process of establishing goals and identifying the necessary steps for the achievement of those goals. There is no single right way to go about financial planning, but a good process might look like the following:

- A. Taking a financial inventory
- B. Assessing your personal situation
- C. Establishing long range goals
- D. Providing for immediate needs
- E. Establishing an investment strategy
- F. Regularly reviewing your status

We will take a brief look at each of these.

A. Taking a Financial Inventory

The first step in financial planning is knowing and understanding your current financial status. This involves listing everything you own and determining the total value of your assets. Then, by subtracting your debts from this figure, you can determine your net worth. Figure 1.1 shows an example of how a typical family's finances, or statement of net worth, might look.

You do this not just to determine the total figure but also in order to analyze the separate sections of the statement. How much debt do you have in relation to your total net worth? How well diversified are your investments? Do you have adequate funds available on short notice in case of an emergency? We will discuss these questions later, and the financial inventory gives you information you need to analyze such issues carefully.

B. Assessing Your Personal Situation

No single financial plan or retirement plan can work for everyone because each family and individual have a different set of circumstances. You need to think carefully about your personal needs in assessing your own situation.

If you know you are going to inherit $5 million, you may not need to worry as much as others about saving part of every paycheck. On the other hand, if you have elderly parents or a handicapped relative who depend on you for financial support, you may need to be more frugal than others with equal income.

If your daughter wants to become a physician and your son an automobile mechanic, the estimated costs of education will be very different for the two. If you love your work and want to continue at it to the age of 70, your retirement planning will be very different than for the person who wants to retire at 55.

These are the kinds of questions involved in assessing your personal situation. No one can answer these but you, and that is why every financial plan must be unique and reflect the special concerns of the individual involved.

C. Establishing Long Range Goals

Most individuals have certain long range goals that must be built into a financial plan. The most common of these are:
1. purchasing a home
2. providing for children's college education
3. starting a business
4. purchasing a vacation home
5. providing for retirement

JOHN AND MARY SAVER
123 THRIFTY STREET
SECURITY VILLAGE, USA

Use Assets				**Debts**			
Auto I		$	8,000	Mortgage		$	45,200
Auto II			4,000	Credit Cards			1,400
House			150,000	Auto I Loan			3,000
Furniture			20,000				
Personal Items			10,000	Total Debts		$	49,600
Boat			8,000				
Coin Collection			4,000				
		$	204,000				

Investment Assets

Equities

Growth Fund	$	8,100	
Internat. Fund		3,200	
100 Sh Gen Mot		4,300	
50 Sh IBM		6,300	
	$	21,900	48.5%

Bonds

Muni Bond Fund	$	5,300	11.7%

Cash and Cash Equivalents

Checking Account	$	2,000	
Certi. of Deposit		8.000	
Life Ins. Cash Val.		1,000	
	$	11,000	24.3%

Real Estate

Limited Part.	$	5,000	11.1%

Precious Metals

Gold Bullion	$	2,000	4.4%

Net Worth
(Total Assets Less Debt)

$ 199,600

Total Investment Assets	$	45,200	100.0%

Total Debts and Net Worth

Total Assets	$	249,200			$	249,200

Figure 1.1. Statement of Net Worth and Asset Diversification

Any or all of these may be a part of your financial plan. Your plan must estimate the costs of these (allowing for future inflation) and build those costs into your annual budgets. Such plans will need to be adjusted periodically as your goals change.

D. Providing for Immediate Needs

You will need to establish a budget that meets your immediate needs and also sets funds aside to achieve your long range goals. Some people set very detailed budgets and discipline themselves to adhere carefully to them. Others are much more general in their budgeting. We will not try to provide a detailed discussion of budgeting here. There are good books available which do that.

We would just remind you of several items you must be sure to include among your immediate needs. You should have an emergency fund to meet living expenses in case of a sudden loss of job, serious illness or other unexpected loss of income. Generally an amount equal to between two and six months living expenses is adequate. If you are a tenured professor at a university, your job security may be good enough that a two-month emergency fund is adequate. If your job security is less secure (maybe you are an untenured faculty member in a discipline with declining enrollments, or worse yet, a coach with a losing record!) your emergency fund should be nearer the six-month figure.

This does not mean these funds should be kept in your checking account but just that they should be available on short notice. You might place them in a savings account, money market fund or short-term certificate of deposit.

Your planning for immediate needs should also include provision for insurance. How much you need depends on your financial condition, personal health, number of dependents, amount of insurance provided by your employer, etc. You will want to do some personal homework and perhaps get some professional assistance to help you decide how much insurance you need.

E. Establishing an Investment Strategy

Perhaps the most important step in the financial planning process is establishing an investment strategy. This includes determining your risk tolerance level (do you lay awake at night and worry if you own common stocks?) and your investment preferences (do you have the carpentry and plumbing skills that will help you in owning rental real estate?).

The fundamental principle for any investment strategy is *diversification.* No other investment principle is more important. Whatever your level of risk tolerance or your investment skills or preferences, there is no single investment so good that it should constitute your entire portfolio. A diversified portfolio might include domestic stocks, foreign stocks, corporate bonds, government bonds, real estate and cash.

As we discuss later, each of these investments is available to you in the various options offered (or to be offered) by TIAA-CREF. The primary purpose of this book is to help you decide how to select among the TIAA-CREF options, and when and how to switch among them, to create an investment strategy that will meet your retirement goals.

Figure 1.2 illustrates the process of building a diversified investment portfolio. Figure 1.3 provides more detailed information on the investments which are appropriate for each of the categories shown in Figure 1.2. Note that the foundation at the bottom of the investment pyramid begins with the items already identified—meeting immediate needs, including the creation of an emergency fund and an insurance program. The higher steps of the pyramid show the ingredients to be used in a diversified portfolio.

```
                          Speculation

                       Higher Risk
                       Investments

         P      Equities (stocks)
         o
    B    r      Bonds
    a    t
    s    f      Cash and Cash Equivalents
    i    o
    c    l      Real Estate
         i
         o      Precious Metals

    Financial Basics
        Basic needs—food, shelter, clothing
        Protection and insurance plan
        Emergency fund
```

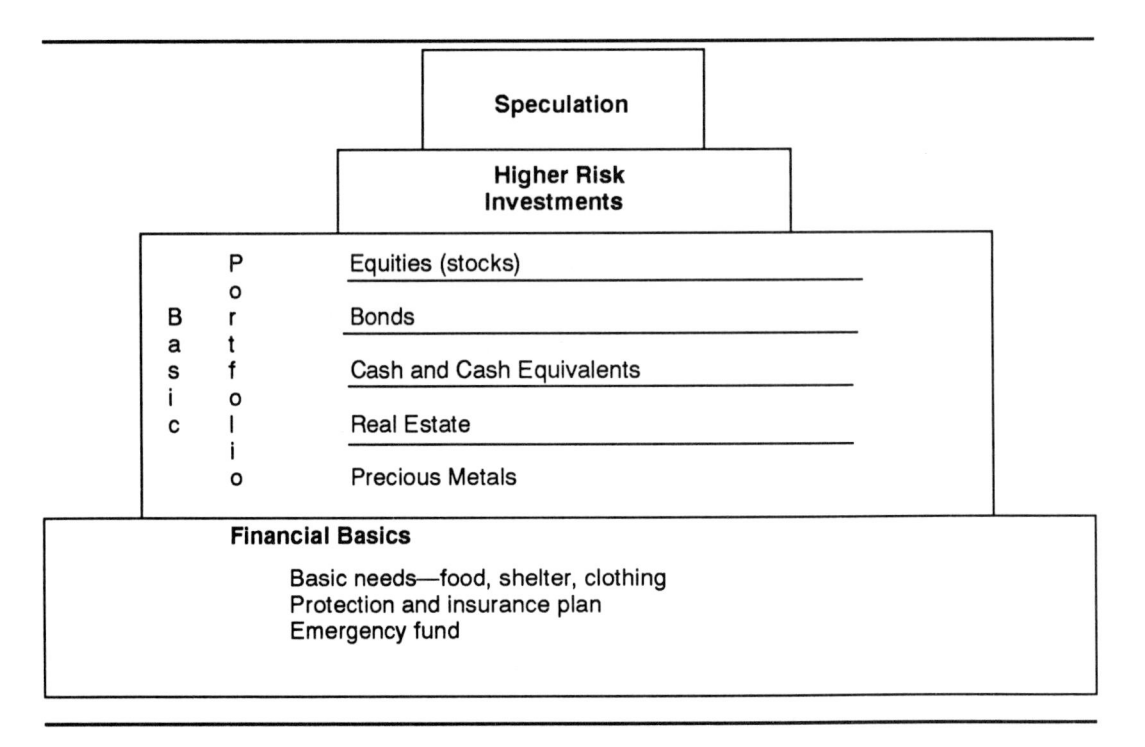

Figure 1.2. The Investment Pyramid

1. Financial Basics
    Provision for basic needs—food, shelter, clothing
    Protection and insurance plan
    Emergency fund
2. Basic Investment Portfolio
    Equities
        Common stocks
        Preferred stocks
        Stock mutual funds
        Futures and options (when used as a hedge)
        Your own business
    Bonds
        Corporate bonds
        U.S. Government bonds
        Municipal bonds
        Foreign bonds (Eurobonds, etc.)
        Bond mutual funds
    Cash and Cash Equivalents
        Checking accounts
        Savings accounts
        Certificates of deposit
        Money market funds
        U.S. Treasury bills (short term)
    Real Estate
        Commercial and residential rental property
        Vacant Land
        Real estate partnerships and syndications
        Real estate mutual funds
        Real estate investment trusts (REIT's)
    Precious Metals
        Bullion
        Precious metal certificates
        Rare coins
        Mining stocks (you may prefer to consider these as equities)
3. Higher Risk Investments
    Most of above with high risk, high return possibilities
    Examples—high beta stocks, "junk bonds," aggressive growth mutual funds, foreign stocks and bonds and highly leveraged real estate investments
4. Speculation
    Investments in which you can afford to lose *all* of your investment
    Examples—penny stocks, foreign mining stocks, options, commodities, currency futures

Figure 1.3. Investment Pyramid Categories

Most investors will never get to the high risk and speculative types of investments. These categories are for you only if you have a very high risk tolerance and if you can afford to lose every penny of the money you place in these investments. Certainly speculative investments are not appropriate for a portfolio designed to meet retirement needs.

F. Monitoring and Reviewing Your Status

A final step in your financial planning process should be a regular review of your plan. While you may want to monitor your investments weekly or monthly (depending on how active you want to be in investment management), a comprehensive review of your entire financial plan need be done only once or twice a year. If you are a faculty member and function on a typical university academic calendar, a review each summer and/or at the Christmas break will be adequate in most cases.

A review should consider whether your goals are still appropriate. Has the health of a family wage-earner changed? Has a child changed his or her plans about whether to go to college? Have you or your spouse received a promotion, a major salary increase or (hopefully not!) been fired? Have your plans about starting a business, buying a summer cottage or retiring at a given age changed? Changes in items such as these may necessitate adjustments in your financial goals.

A review should also consider whether your investments are still appropriate for your long range financial goals. Some investment decisions are made on the basis of current economic, monetary or stock market conditions. Other decisions, however, may be independent of such immediate considerations. A fifty-five year old, for example, will probably want a smaller percentage of his retirement portfolio subject to stock market risk than a twenty-five year old regardless of current economic conditions.

Retirement Planning

Retirement planning is one aspect of financial planning. It is unique in that it is almost always the longest of your long range goals. Meeting your retirement goals will come later in life than purchasing a home, starting a business or providing your children a college education.

Retirement planning has at least two important advantages. One is that it is truly long range. You can build an investment portfolio over a long period of time. The impact of any individual upturn or downturn in the economy will be minimized because of the long term nature of the investments.

The other advantage is that retirement funds can be invested on a tax-deferred basis, and they can grow and earn income on that basis. Money that goes into a retirement fund like TIAA-CREF or into supplemental retirement accounts (SRA's) such as 403 (b) programs, consists of "before tax" dollars. In addition, the income on these funds is tax sheltered. No tax need be paid until funds are withdrawn from the retirement account.

The major difficulty with retirement planning is *uncertainty*. Since it is impossible to predict future inflation rates, there is no way to know exactly how much you will need to save for retirement. You can estimate how much income you will have at retirement, but it is more difficult to estimate how much a given amount of money will buy in the future.

Another uncertainty associated with retirement is life expectancy. You cannot know how long you or your spouse will live. As explained in Chapter 8, you do not have to worry about this so far as your TIAA-CREF or similar retirement programs are concerned. You will have the opportunity at the time of retirement to use your TIAA-CREF funds to purchase an annuity which will guarantee you an income for life. You will be able to choose among several options which enable you to guarantee an income to the surviving spouse when one of you dies or to assure an income for a specific number of years.

There are procedures that will enable you to make reasonably accurate estimates about your financial needs at retirement. This involves estimating what you believe future inflation rates will be, what your annual income will be and what rate of return your retirement funds will earn between now and retirement.

In spite of the uncertainties of retirement planning, the opportunities to establish a long range investment program and take advantage of tax deferral make it possible for the average person to assure a comfortable, financially secure retirement.

Bibliography

Block, Stanley B., Peavy, John W., and Thornton, John H., *Personal Financial Management,* Harper & Row, 1988.

Brosterman, Robert, *The Complete Estate Planning Guide.* McGraw-Hill, 1982.

Gitman, Lawrence J., and Joehnk, Michael D., *Personal Financial Planning,* Dryden Press, 1987.

Tobias, Andrew, *The Only Other Investment Guide You'll Ever Need,* Simon and Schuster, 1987.

Vicker, Ray, *The Dow Jones-Irwin Guide to Retirement Planning,* Dow Jones-Irwin, 1987.

Chapter 2

TIAA-CREF and Other Options

For more than 70 years, Teachers Insurance and Annuity (TIAA) has been the primary organization for providing a retirement program for college and university faculty and staff in the United States. TIAA provides a stable fixed income to participants. For over 35 years, College Retirement Equities Fund (CREF) has operated in conjunction with TIAA to enable faculty to invest a portion of their retirement funds in the stock market, providing them with the opportunity to participate in the advances (and declines!) in the market.

The investment strategies discussed in this book can be used with the retirement funds of many companies, not just TIAA-CREF. Today many universities provide their faculty and staff opportunities to choose among several investment firms, of which TIAA-CREF is only one. Even if you place your retirement funds with a different investment organization, the strategies outlined here can be used to maximize the return on your money. Because TIAA-CREF is still the most widely used of all investment firms among institutions of higher education, it is useful to provide some additional background on that organization's structure and activities.

History

TIAA was founded in 1918 by the Carnegie Foundation for the Advancement of Teaching and the Carnegie Corporation. It was incorporated in New York as a non-profit, legal-reserve life insurance and annuity company. Its purpose was to provide a secure, well managed retirement program for the nation's college and university faculty members. TIAA provided the additional advantage of portability. Since college teaching is by nature a mobile profession, TIAA offered the opportunity for faculty to take their retirement benefits with them as they moved from one institution to another. Prior to this time most faculty who had any retirement plan at all were limited to the plan of one institution or, in many cases, the state retirement system of the given state in which their university was located.

TIAA also offered individual colleges and universities the opportunity to get out (or stay out) of the business of managing retirement funds. It could offer economies of scale, the strength of a national system and the advantages which came because of the initial financing and support from Carnegie. In addition to offering retirement plans, it also offered life, disability and medical insurance. Our emphasis in this book is on its retirement programs.

The organization invests its funds primarily in loans, bonds, mortgages and income-producing real estate. While such investments are not without some risk, they tend to provide a high degree of safety and stability over a long period of time. Therefore, TIAA is able to assure participants a stable, fixed income in retirement.

CREF is a separate New York non-profit corporation established in 1952. It was organized for the purpose of providing participants the opportunity to invest some or all of their retirement funds in equities, mainly publicly held common stocks traded on the major stock exchanges. This gave participants access to much more volatile investment instruments, with the opportunity for much greater return but also the risk of greater loss. The total amount of CREF accumulation in the participant's account at the time of retirement will depend on the performance of the market during the participant's working years and how he or she used investment strategies to maximize the return on the account. The strategies discussed in the following chapters are designed to assist in that effort.

Recent Developments

Although occasional changes were made, TIAA-CREF operated with much stability from the 1950's to the 1970's. Faculty could choose how to allocate their retirement contributions between TIAA and CREF. The most common pattern was for faculty to allocate 50% of their retirement funds to each, but the entire array of possibilities was available to them. More conservative faculty would place a larger percentage in TIAA while more venturesome participants would put more into CREF.

In addition to deciding how to allocate retirement fund contributions, participants could also move accumulated lump sums from CREF to TIAA. They did not, however, have the higher risk option of moving funds from TIAA to CREF. Once funds were invested in TIAA, they stayed there.

As time passed, especially in the 1980's, a variety of criticisms began to be directed at TIAA-CREF. Some of the criticism was from individuals, some from major universities such as Stanford and Johns Hopkins, and some from national higher education associations. The National Association of College and University Business Officers (NACUBO) even appointed a special committee to study TIAA-CREF and make recommendations for improvements. TIAA-CREF also appointed its own committee, the TIAA-CREF Ad Hoc Committee on Goals and Objectives, to look at issues raised and make recommendations.

Some of the major concerns which have been raised through the years included:

1. There were only two investment options, the "fixed income" TIAA option and the "variable income" CREF option. (This criticism is now being addressed, and the additional options available are the major subject of this book.)
2. The flexibility permitted the participant was too limited. As noted above, funds could only be moved from CREF to TIAA, not in the other direction.
3. There was no opportunity to transfer funds to other investment companies which the participant might believe to have a better investment record or to be more consistent with the participant's personal investment objectives. Retirement funds going to the TIAA-CREF organization had to stay there.
4. At the time of retirement, the participant was limited to retirement payout options offered by TIAA-CREF. The retiree could not "roll over" his or her funds into an annuity or payout program offered by some other company.
5. The ability of the retiree to take a lump sum payment at the time of retirement was very limited, in most cases to just 10% of the funds in the account.

There have been other issues raised but these are the ones of most concern to the average participant. TIAA-CREF responded to the criticisms with a variety of new programs and services. Some of these changes have already been implemented, and some will come in the future.

One of the most important actions has been the approval of seven new investment alternatives from which participants may choose for the investment of their funds. Not all of them were created immediately. Rather, they will be phased in over time. The planned new funds are:

1. *CREF Money Market Fund.* This option was placed in effect in 1988. Funds are invested in very short term investment instruments which provide a minimum of risk. This will be a good place for participants to "park" money until they decide where it should be invested.
2. *CREF Bond Fund.* This fund would invest in bonds rather than stocks. It would have some price volatility, but that volatility would be caused mainly by changes in and the general level of interest rates.
3. *CREF Balanced Fund.* This fund would be designed to have a balanced portfolio of different kinds of investments. It could invest in stocks, bonds, money market, instruments and perhaps even real estate (depending on how its objectives are stated when it is actually established). This diversification should reduce risk for the investor.
4. *CREF Actively Managed Equities Fund.* This stock market fund will be more actively traded, have more volatility and involve more risk than the original CREF fund. The fund is designed for the more aggressive investor and those who want to diversify by placing a portion of their money in a higher-risk/higher-opportunity-for-return type of investment instrument.
5. *CREF Passive Equities Fund.* This fund is designed to reflect the general movements, up and down, of the stock market as a whole. This type of fund is called an "index fund." It should neither outperform nor underperform the general market over an extended period of time.
6. *CREF International Equities Funds.* Investors who want to place a portion of their money in the stocks of foreign countries may use this fund. It will give participants the opportunity to get greater diversification in their portfolios. It may also have somewhat greater volatility because it will be subject not only to stock market fluctuations but also to the fluctuations in currency values.
7. *TIAA Fund.* This is the original TIAA Fund but with a major revision. Plans are now under way to allow participants to transfer money out of TIAA as well as into it. Questions such as what portion of the funds can be moved out and whether "old money" as well as "new money" can be moved are still being worked out by TIAA-CREF.

These new funds which are planned will give the TIAA-CREF participant much more flexibility in investment strategies once they are all available.

They also place much more responsibility on the individual. In the past the only question the investor had to answer was, "What percentage of my funds should go into TIAA, and what percentage should go into CREF?" Now the investor must decide how to allocate monthly contributions among several options, and he or she must also consider whether switching existing accumulations among the various options is advantageous.

The individual participant, of course, may decide to do nothing. The investor, confused by the array of new options, can ignore the issue and just leave the allocation divided between TIAA and CREF as it has been for years. There may be nothing wrong with this approach, but it does mean that the participant chooses to ignore options which could significantly improve income and life style during retirement. It would be like ignoring the interstate highway system because the map showing exits, entrances, overpasses, cloverleafs, etc. seems so confusing. It would be possible to drive across the nation without using the interstate highway system, but the driver pays a price, including the cost of lost opportunities, for doing so.

This book is designed to help the average TIAA-CREF participant through the confusion of investment options and strategies. However much or little interest you have in investments, there are parts of this book that should help you improve your retirement planning and increase your retirement income.

Retirement Income

At the time of retirement, the TIAA-CREF participant's funds become the foundation for providing income during retirement years. Unlike many retirement programs, you cannot project with great accuracy what your retirement income will be if you are still a decade or more away from retirement. This is because TIAA-CREF provides what is called a "defined contribution plan" rather than a "defined income plan."

A "defined contribution plan" is one which states specifically what the contributions will be. You may be in a plan, for example, where you and your employer each contribute a certain percentage of your monthly salary for retirement. Contributions by employers and employees need not be equal. Your plan might call for you to contribute 5% and for your employer to contribute an amount equal to 10% of your income. The possible combinations are limitless.

As you will note, these plans spell out exactly what the contributions will be, but the amount of retirement income cannot be projected as specifically. This is because retirement income will be determined by the performance of investments between now and the time of retirement. TIAA will guarantee a certain minimum amount, but the actual payments to the retiree are usually considerably above the guaranteed amount. This is because income received by TIAA on its investments tends to be higher than the very conservative interest rate assumptions used in projecting the guaranteed minimum. CREF retirement payments will depend on the performance of the stock market and may vary greatly from estimated projections. As you can imagine, predicting retirement income becomes even more difficult if retirement money is invested in five or six different options rather than only one or two.

The individual retiree also influences the amount of retirement payments by selecting which payment option he or she prefers. The unmarried retiree who wants to guarantee a retirement income only during his or her own lifetime will receive higher monthly payments than the married individual who wants to guarantee a lifetime income for both retiree and spouse, whichever lives the longest. A retiree who chooses a plan that provides for an annual inflation adjustment must accept lower monthly payments in the early years of retirement. These options are discussed in more detail in Chapter 8.

Assuming the participant has not taken the very conservative approach of allocating all retirement contributions to TIAA, retirement income will be affected by the performance of the invested funds during the participant's working years. Therefore, wise use of prudent investment strategies, such as those explained in this book, should help enhance retirement income.

Supplementary Retirement Annuities

Your employer may provide an opportunity to have a supplementary retirement annuity (SRA). An SRA is a voluntary contribution made by an employee to go into a retirement fund to supplement the basic retirement program. An employee's basic retirement is usually not voluntary; employees must participate in their employer's general plan whether they want to or not.

TIAA-CREF provides opportunities for SRA contributions to go into the same investment options that are available for the contributions to the basic investment plan. One advantage of an SRA is that money placed in such a plan is withheld from the employer's salary *before taxes* and placed directly in the SRA. Also, as with the basic plan, income earned on the contributions accumulates on a tax-deferred basis. Taxes on both the contributions and the earnings are, therefore, deferred until the funds are ultimately received during retirement.

SRA's are subject to a variety of legal limitations, including contribution limits and restrictions on how and at what age withdrawals may be made. Those interested in an SRA should review the restrictions before deciding to make contributions to the plan.

If you decide to contribute to an SRA, you will want to coordinate your strategy for SRA investments with the strategy for your other retirement funds. As an example, you might use a higher risk strategy for your SRA funds than for funds in your basic retirement program.

Other (Non-TIAA-CREF) Retirement Plans

Some institutions which have TIAA-CREF retirement plans are now offering other retirement plans as well. The participant is provided the alternative of using the TIAA-CREF investment options or the options offered by the other companies.

We make no attempt here to evaluate these alternatives or to suggest that TIAA-CREF is either better or worse than plans offered by other investment companies. We do want to emphasize that the investment strategies discussed here can be used with TIAA-CREf or with the investment plans of other companies.

Our analysis focuses on TIAA-CREF options, and our strategies are based on the options which that organization now makes available or plans to make available in the future. Once you understand the strategies, you can adjust them to fit the options made available by other retirement plans. For example, if you develop an investment strategy that makes use of a bond fund and an international stock fund, that strategy should be appropriate whether you are using the funds sponsored by TIAA-CREF or similar funds made available by another investment firm.

Bibliography

Final Report of the Ad Hoc Committee on TIAA-CREF, National Association of College and University Business Officers, 1985.

The Participant, TIAA-CREF, February, 1988. Contains several articles on new options and plans for the future.

"Pension Companies Agree to Ease Rules on Funds Transfer," *Chronicle of Higher Education,* January 4, 1989, pp. A1, A13–15.

Report of the TIAA-CREF Ad Hoc Committee on Goals and Objectives, TIAA-CREF, 1985.

"Summary of the Report of the TIAA-CREF Ad Hoc Committee on Goals and Objectives," *The Participant,* TIAA-CREF, April, 1985.

Chapter 3

Choosing an Investment Strategy

How simple it used to be! Many TIAA-CREF participants just split their retirement contributions evenly between the two and forgot about it. Some very conservative investors put all their contributions in TIAA. Now it is no longer so simple.

In developing a plan for your retirement contributions today, you have two important questions to answer:

1. What investment strategy (or strategies) should I use? Alternative strategies are explained in Chapters 4–7. You may decide on one appropriate strategy for all of your investment funds. Some may want to use more than one strategy, perhaps a conservative strategy for your basic retirement plan and a higher risk strategy for your SRA. You can even use more than one strategy within your basic plan, perhaps a low risk strategy for two-thirds of your money and a higher risk strategy for the other third.
2. Which of the funds available should I use in implementing my strategy or strategies? As noted in Chapter 2, when TIAA-CREF completes its plans, there will be eight investment funds available, as follows:

    TIAA (the original fund, as revised to allow transfers out)
    CREF (the original CREF fund)
    CREF Money Market Fund
    CREF Bond Fund
    CREF Balanced Fund
    CREF Actively Managed Equity Fund
    CREF Passive Equities Fund
    CREF International Equities Fund

It is obvious that some of these will involve more risk than others. The Money Market Fund will offer virtually no risk. The Bond Fund and

Balanced Fund should offer relatively low risk. The Actively Managed Equities Fund and the International Equities Fund will be relatively higher in risk.

The variety of combinations available to the investor will be almost limitless. You might use a simple strategy involving little time (perhaps from chapter IV) but implement it using some of the higher risk funds. A young participant who is willing to take some risk and to spend some time working with his investments may want to use one of the strategies that will necessitate the use of his or her computer (from Chapter VII) and invest in some of the higher risk funds. The participant who is both risk averse and has little interest in financial matters can choose a simple strategy (from Chapters IV or V) and invest only in the more conservative funds.

The first step in deciding on appropriate strategies and funds is to consider one's own personal and financial status. Let us create four mythical TIAA-CREF participants, who have characteristics typical of many others, and then review some of the questions they need to ask themselves:

Al Adams, 35 years old, is an associate professor of electrical engineering. He is married and the father of two children. His wife does not work outside the home. He is very computer literate and is interested in financial matters.

Barbara Baker, 40, is a professor of accounting. She is a single parent and is the sole support for two teenage children. In addition to her faculty duties, she does quite a lot of accounting and tax consultation work.

Calvin Clark, 28, is an assistant professor of art. His wife is a nurse, and they have one child. He has little interest in or knowledge of financial matters. He is aware that he will at some point in the future inherit a rather large amount of money from his parents.

Doreen Davis, 50, is director of research for a national association of school administrators. Her husband is a high school history teacher. She is interested in maximizing her retirement income, but she feels at her age she should not take excessive risk.

Each of these individuals will have a different approach to handling their retirement funds. We will look at some of the concerns they must consider in deciding on an investment strategy appropriate to their own situation.

Personal Situation

In beginning to think about retirement planning, one should first consider some very personal questions. How old are you? A 30 year old can usually be more venturesome in investment strategy than a 55 year old. One would expect Calvin Clark to be able to assume more risk than Doreen Davis.

Individuals should consider their particular financial situation and financial obligations. A young faculty member whose parents have established a million dollar trust fund for her may not need to worry much about retirement. If, in contrast, she knows that not only does she have no independent financial resources but she will be responsible for helping support a physically handicapped brother, she will need to be very careful in her retirement planning.

Family situation is always important. In a one income family with children in the home, like that of Al Adams, it becomes crucial for the income earner to take a prudent approach to the investment of retirement funds. In a two income family, where both incomes are relatively high and both are contributing to retirement programs, the couple may deliberately plan to use an aggressive, high risk strategy with one of the retirement plans and a more conservative approach with the other.

A very significant question to ask is at what age you plan to retire. University faculty are unique in that for many of them their work, especially their research, is the central activity of their life. They may choose to work until 70 or even longer. Others, of course, may want to retire much earlier.

Many institutions today have early retirement incentives, and participants should be aware of how such plans affect their particular situation. We know a university vice-president who was quite well paid by university standards. At 60, he checked to see what his income would be if he retired. He discovered that, when he considered his institution's incentive for early retirement as well as his regular retirement, his total retirement income would be only about $7,000 less than his salary. He was working full time for about $7,000 a year! He soon decided to retire.

There are several books and even computer programs which will assist you in projecting income needs at the time of retirement. These depend on assumptions made about future inflation levels, tax rates, salary increases, etc., so they provide only approximate projections at best. TIAA-CREF will help you estimate your future income, but these projections too are only approximations.

Risk Tolerance

A fundamental aspect of any investment program, whether for retirement or other purposes, is risk tolerance. There are at least two aspects of the risk tolerance question: (1) how much risk an investor can tolerate *financially* and (2) how much risk an investor can tolerate *psychologically*.

Risk tolerance refers to how much risk one should take in implementing an investment program. This depends primarily on one's financial status. The young woman with the million dollar trust fund would ordinarily have a higher risk tolerance than the individual with no extra resources and with responsibility for supporting a physically handicapped brother. Al Adams and Barbara Baker are both the only income providers in their families, and this will reduce their risk tolerance in comparison with Calvin Clark and Doreen Davis, both of whom are part of two income families.

One's financial ability to accept risk is not the only question. Some people are just not *psychologically* suited to high risk tolerance. We know an individual with large investments in the stock market who never worries or loses a minute of sleep however much the market fluctuates. This same person used to own income-producing real estate, and he fretted and worried unceasingly whenever he had a vacancy or other problem. He was correct to get out of real estate and into the market because he had little psychological risk tolerance for real estate but no similar problem with stocks. If he wants real estate in his portfolio, for diversification purposes, he should buy real estate partnerships or real estate mutual funds.

Others have little psychological risk tolerance for the stock market. They may even be wealthy and their life style not at all at risk, but they nevertheless panic and worry with every slight downturn in their price of their stock. However financially able they may be to tolerate risk, they are not psychologically able to do so in the stock market.

There is no magic thermometer that measures one's level of risk tolerance, especially on the psychological side. Each investor must consider his or her own situation and decide how much risk tolerance is appropriate for retirement planning. The person whose risk tolerance is low will invest mainly in TIAA and the more conservative CREF funds. The person with high risk tolerance will want to put at least a portion of investment funds in the more aggressive CREF funds and probably use one of the more activist strategies outlined in the following chapters.

Interest and Competence in Investing

If you are a TIAA-CREF participant, it is likely that in past years you spent very little time making decisions about investment policies concerning your retirement funds. You will be able to continue that pattern in the future if you want to. You can make a very basic decision and then almost forget about investment planning if you so desire.

The advantage of the new TIAA-CREF funds is that participants now have the opportunity to take a much more active role in the investment of their retirement funds if they choose to do so. As discussed in Chapters 4 and 5, there are investment strategies available for the person who wants to spend no more than a few minutes a year on the subject. Later chapters define strategies for those willing to spend up to an hour or more a week on investment matters.

Going back to our four participants, we note that Al Adams, an electrical engineer, is familiar with computers and also interested in financial matters. A strategy involving computer analysis and a time commitment of an hour a week or more will be appropriate for him. In contrast, Calvin Clark, our young artist, has little interest in the markets and probably won't want to devote more than a few minutes a year on investments.

Time Commitment

Finally, an individual must decide how much time he or she *wants* to devote to the active management of retirement funds. This decision is crucial in the selection of appropriate investment strategies. There are individuals with both competence and interest in financial matters who may decide not to commit significant amounts of time to investment matters.

Barbara Baker, our 40 year old accounting professor, should certainly have the competence to make intelligent decisions about investment matters. You will remember, though, that she spends much of her spare time doing tax and accounting consulting. As a matter of personal choice, she may prefer to spend an extra hour a week on her consulting business rather than devote it to investment management. This has nothing to do with competence; it is just personal preference.

It is not an all-or-nothing matter. Remember that Professor Baker is a single parent, and she probably does not want to take too much risk through using an aggressive investment strategy. She could select a strategy that involves a time commitment of no more than 15 minutes to an hour each month. This would give her the opportunity to exercise some management over her retirement funds while still allowing her to devote most of her time to her consulting.

Investment Strategies: Some Examples

There are no precision instruments for measuring such personal characteristics as risk tolerance, investment competence, interest in investing, etc. There certainly are no such instruments for evaluating one's personal situation. If you are attempting some self-evaluation in preparation for developing an investment strategy, remember that much of your effort will be subjective.

There are, of course, some broad generalizations that usually apply. Most people should assume less risk as they get older, and they should, therefore, shift to more conservative strategies as they get nearer retirement. A person whose personal situation requires him to carry special financial burdens such as supporting parents is likely to want a low risk strategy. A young couple, both of whom have good salaries and no plans for children can afford to accept much higher risk if they are willing to devote a little time to their investments.

Let us look again at our four participants and see how they might select appropriate investment strategies. Keep in mind that there is no *one right strategy,* but there are some which will be much more appropriate than others.

Al Adams. Al will probably be the most aggressive of our four investors for several reasons. At 35, he is young and has time to recover if he suffers some losses. Since his discipline is engineering, he can expect to receive a higher average salary over his career than many of his colleagues in other academic disciplines. He is interested in financial matters and has a knowledge of computers so we assume he is willing to spend up to an hour a week on his investments.

A good plan for Al would be to have two investment strategies. Strategy I would be a moderate to low risk strategy to be used for 50% of his TIAA-CREF funds. He can use one of the dollar averaging strategies selected from Chapter 5. You will learn in Chapter 5 why dollar averaging strategies work best with more volatile investments. Because Al wants this strategy to involve only moderate risk, he can pick two funds which offer volatility and some risk—the Passive Equities Fund, which should move up and down at about the same rate as the stock market as a whole, and the Bond Fund, which should move up and down in response to changes in interest rates.

Al's Strategy II will be higher risk. He will select one of the computer assisted technical strategies from Chapter 6. He will maintain data on his computer, which he will update once a week, a process that will take only a few minutes weekly. He will then look at the data and switch among several funds on the basis of what his technical strategy tells him to do. To implement this strategy, he will use some of the higher risk funds—the Actively Managed Equities Fund and the International Equities Fund. His strategy may call for him to switch at certain times from an equity fund, such as those mentioned, to a money market fund, and for this purpose he will use the CREF Money Market Fund.

How, you may ask, can Al allocate his funds between two different strategies? It is fairly simple. With the availability of the new funds, he can allocate funds to several of them, so that 50% of his monthly contributions go to his Strategy I funds and the other 50% to his Strategy II funds. Of course, the allocations will never stay at exactly 50% in each because each of the funds will fluctuate in value on a daily basis. Al will then use his strategies to shift funds based on his strategies in hopes of maximizing his return.

As Al gets older, he will probably want to move toward a more conservative investment plan. At age 45 or 50 he may want to shift so that two-thirds of his money is invested through the more conservative Strategy I and only one-third through the higher risk Strategy II. At age 55, he can make another adjustment and leave only one-fourth of his funds to be invested on the basis of Strategy II.

Barbara Baker. Barbara, as an accountant, is likely to have the competence to implement and manage a sophisticated investment strategy. She has indicated, though, that she is not interested in devoting a lot of time to her TIAA-CREF investments. She prefers to use her time in her consulting business. As a single parent with the financial responsibility for a family, she will also prefer a rather conservative investment strategy.

Barbara can choose one of the dollar averaging strategies from Chapter 5. She can do this by devoting no more than 15–30 minutes a month to it. If she desires (although it is certainly not necessary), she can combine her dollar averaging strategy with a permanent allocation strategy from Chapter 4. This latter strategy can be implemented in no more than an hour once a year.

To implement this combined strategy, Barbara will invest in three different funds to provide diversification. She can use the Actively Managed Equity Fund to get some of her money into the stock market. Second, she can use the Bond Fund to assure some stable income with somewhat less risk. Third, she can use TIAA to diversify into other kinds of investments and to get the safety and stability traditionally provided by TIAA.

Calvin Clark. Calvin, our 28 year old assistant professor of art appears to have a contradictory situation to deal with. On the one hand, he has no interest in investments and desires to devote little time to the subject. On the other hand, his young age and the fact that he will inherit a large amount of money should give him a high risk tolerance. He is a good candidate for an aggressive, high risk strategy.

Is there an investment strategy appropriate for his unique situation? Yes, Calvin can take advantage of a plan that will meet his needs and involve little time commitment. First, he can choose a permanent allocation strategy from Chapter 4. Then he can implement this strategy by using four funds—Actively Managed Equities Fund, International Equities Fund, Bond Fund, and TIAA. The Actively Managed and International Equities Funds are consistent with Calvin's ability to accept a higher level of risk. The Bond and TIAA funds provided needed diversification for his retirement money.

Calvin can use this approach by devoting not more than one hour a year and having virtually no knowledge of or interest in investment matters. Let us assume, as explained in Chapter 4, that Calvin wants 25% of his money in each of the four funds. First, he tells his university that his monthly retirement contributions to TIAA-CREF should be divided equally among the four funds. Next, once each year, perhaps during the summer after he has received his June 30 quarterly statement from TIAA-CREF, Calvin will sit down and calculate the percentage of his total investment which is in each fund. He will then calculate how much he must switch from some funds to others to restore his desired allocation. The rationale for doing this is explained in Chapter 4.

That one hour per year is the only time Calvin needs to devote to the matter. He probably will not do as well as Al, who is devoting time each week to his computer analysis; nevertheless, Calvin's one hour annual time commitment is likely to give him a significantly better return over the whole period of his working years than doing nothing at all and just taking his chances.

Doreen Davis. Doreen, at age 50, cannot afford to be reckless in her choice of strategies. Still, she and her husband both have secure jobs, and she is interested in devoting time to maximizing her retirement income. As a research director, we can assume that she has the ability to collect data and analyze it.

Doreen may decide, like Al, to use two separate investment strategies. She will manage 60% of her money on the basis of one of the more sophisticated dollar averaging strategies from Chapter 5, using the Balanced Fund and the Passive Equities Fund to get a balance of market volatility and diversity.

The other 40% will be invested based on one of the strategies from Chapter 6, making use of economic indicators. She can use her research capability to implement this strategy. Strategies based on economic indicators often use various kinds of investment vehicles, so she will use three funds—Actively Managed Securities Fund, Bond Fund and TIAA. These three will provide her the diversification of, respectively, stocks, bonds and real estate and related fixed income investments.

One thing we have not considered in Doreen's husband's retirement plan. The two of them may want to handle their retirement plans so that each complements the other. For example, if his plan is a good one with a very conservative investment philosophy and perhaps even a guaranteed monthly amount of income, then Doreen can be more aggressive. She may want to invest all of her retirement, rather than just 60%, in her more aggressive economic indicators strategy.

To Summarize

We have attempted to describe in this chapter the process an individual will go through in developing an investment plan for retirement funds. The individual will begin by doing a self-evaluation. This will include analyzing one's personal situation, risk tolerance, investment competence, investment interest and willingness to spend time on investment management. Much of the evaluation will be subjective, but it will help an individual select an appropriate investment strategy or strategies.

The individual must next make the selection of an appropriate strategy or strategies. These can be simple or complex and involve varying amounts of time to implement. Some may require a computer, but most will not.

The participant must then select the appropriate TIAA-CREF funds to use in implementation. It is the combination of the two—appropriate strategy and appropriate funds—which determines how successful the individual will be in providing for retirement. The strategies should be adjusted at various times in one's life as personal factors (marital status, financial condition, age, years until retirement, etc.) change.

Finally, there are two other matters you should keep in mind. First, as noted earlier, not all of the TIAA-CREF fund options described above are actually available at the time of writing this book. Second, your university may make available to you a series of fund options from an investment company other than TIAA-CREF. Your selection of funds will depend on what is available to you at the time of implementation. The strategies discussed throughout this book can be implemented with other funds having similar characteristics. They do not depend on the availability of the specific TIAA-CREF funds mentioned above.

Bibliography

Brimelow, Peter, *The Wall Street Gurus,* Random House, 1986.

Fosback, Norman G., *Stock Market Logic,* Institute for Econometric Research, 1976.

Nichols, Donald R., *Life Cycle Investing,* Dow Jones-Irwin, 1985.

Zweig, Martin, *Winning on Wall Street,* Warner, 1986.

Chapter 4

Asset Allocation Strategies

The next four chapters present a series of investment strategies. You may choose one or more as appropriate for your own use, or you may alter them to adapt them to your special needs and preferences. The strategies are arranged generally from most simple in this chapter to most complex in Chapter VII.

Accumulations and Monthly Allocations: Understanding the Differences

Before we look at special strategies, we will take a moment to dwell on what may seem only too obvious—the difference between *accumulations* (sometimes called accumulated balances) and *allocations*. We do so because we know individuals who have confused the two and have made serious investment errors because of that confusion. Our investment strategies in this and the following chapters are based on changes in either accumulations or monthly allocations, and it is imperative that you know which to use at the appropriate time.

At many universities, a given amount is withheld from the employee's salary each month, and this amount is supplemented by a contribution from the employer. At other institutions, the entire contribution is made by the employer. These retirement funds, whether contributed by the employee, the employer, or both, are sent monthly by the employer to TIAA-CREF.

Each employee must indicate how these contributions are to be allocated among the various funds available. These are what are called the *monthly allocations*. As we have noted, many participants in the past have allocated 50% each to TIAA and CREF. As more investment options become available, the alternatives increase. If there are eight different investment funds, it would theoretically be possible to allocate 1/8 of your monthly contributions to each of the funds. Alternatively, 100% could go into one fund and the other seven could be ignored. In practice, most people are likely to allocate to several funds but probably not to all.

Accumulations, or *accumulated balances,* are the total amounts a participant has in each fund as of a given date. For example, a participant may have allocated 50% of his monthly contributions to TIAA and 50% to CREF for several years. As of December 31, 1987, because of five years of a rising stock market, his CREF accumulations will have grown faster than his TIAA accumulations. His accumulated balances might be $24,000 in CREF and $19,000 in TIAA. If the participant preferred an equal amount in each, he could simply call TIAA-CREF (at 1–800–842–2252) and request that $2500 of his CREF funds be moved to TIAA. He would then have a $21,500 balance in each account. Note that he has made *no change* in his monthly allocations, only in his accumulations.

As you read this and the following chapters, you will see how changes in monthly allocations and accumulations are an integral part of our investment strategies. You will also see why it is essential not to confuse the two.

Permanent Allocation Strategies

Beginning in the 1970's several money managers and investment writers began to concentrate on the concept of *asset allocation* for achieving investment objectives. There were some mutual funds established whose entire investment strategy is based on this philosophy. This investment approach can be divided into two categories—*permanent allocation strategies* and *variable allocation strategies.* We will look first at permanent allocation strategies. These strategies are permanent in that our allocations do not change because of any economic or market conditions. We never change allocations because of what we think will happen to the stock market, interest rates, inflation or other factors.

Equal Allocation Strategy

Equal allocation is the first of our permanent allocation strategies. This strategy is simple to understand and simple to implement. *It can literally be implemented in 30 minutes a year!* This strategy is spelled out in detail in one of the best investment books of the 1980's, *Why the Best-Laid Investment Plans Usually Go Wrong,* by Harry Browne.

While we do not agree with all the conclusions of the book (for example, we are not as optimistic about gold as a long-term investment, we believe Browne has done a very fine job of analyzing the contemporary economic and investment environment and pointing out the shortcomings of many of the current "get rich quick" investment strategies. An investor interested in the underlying philosophy behind this strategy can learn more about it by reading Browne's entire book.

His strategy is a simple one. He recommends dividing one's investment money equally among four different kinds of investments:

> *25% in common stocks*
> *25% in government bonds*
> *25% in cash and cash equivalents*
> *25% in gold*

Once each year the investor shifts balances among the four to adjust them so that each category again equals 25% of the total amount invested.

The idea behind this approach is that different investments do well at different times. Common stocks performed less well than other investments in the early to mid-1970's, but they did better than most other investments in the 1980's. Gold did very well in the late 1970's and early 1980's, but it has trailed most other investments since. This approach is designed to take profits from investments which have done well and move them into other investments when their prices are low.

To illustrate, when gold prices are rising and stock prices are lagging, the process of getting each investment back to 25% would involve selling some gold and using the money to buy stocks at a very good time, i.e. when stock prices are relatively low. Browne says his research indicates that this approach, if applied over the 17 years prior to publication of his book, would have provided an annual compound investment return of 12%.

The equal allocation strategy can be used by TIAA-CREF investors although not precisely as recommended by Browne. The main difference is that TIAA-CREF does not have a fund that invests mainly in gold and/or gold stocks. Also there is no TIAA-CREF fund that invests only in government bonds, but the Bond Fund can be used as a reasonable alternative. To use this approach we would recommend the following funds:

> *TIAA*
> *CREF Actively Managed Equities Fund*
> *CREF Bond Fund*
> *CREF Money Market Fund*

This is similar to the approach outlined above except for the use of TIAA instead of a gold fund. Given the options available, we think this is the best approach. Gold is often seen as a protection against inflation, and since TIAA's holdings include real estate and mortgages, it should provide similar inflation protection.

An investor with somewhat more risk tolerance might use the International Equities Fund instead of TIAA. The equal allocation strategy depends in part on volatility to work, and the International Equities Fund will almost certainly be more volatile than TIAA. This fund will not be as closely related to inflation as TIAA or a gold fund (if one were available), but it does offer both diversification and volatility.

Implementation of this approach is very simple. You need take just two steps:

1. Establish your monthly allocations so that they are distributed as follows:

    25% to TIAA
    25% to CREF Actively Managed Equities Fund
    25% to CREF Bond Fund
    25% to CREF Money Market Fund

2. Once each year, just after you have received a quarterly report from TIAA-CREF, calculate what you need to do to get your allocations back to 25% in account. Then call TIAA-CREF (1–800–842–2252) and adjust your accounts so that each of them once again contains about 25% of your funds. It is not important when you do this so long as you do it at the same time each year.

As an example, let us assume that your June 30 TIAA-CREF statement shows your accumulation balances to be:

TIAA	*$16,000*
CREF Actively Managed Equities Fund	*11,000*
CREF Bond Fund	*18,000*
CREF Money Market Fund	*15,000*
	$60,000

You want $15,000 (25%) in each account, so you can leave your CREF Money Market Fund alone since it contains this amount already. You will call TIAA-CREF and give them directions to make two transfers:

1. Transfer $3000 from your CREF Bond Fund Account to your CREF Actively Managed Equities Account.
2. Transfer $1000 from your TIAA Account to your CREF Actively Managed Equities Account. This assumes that TIAA-CREF has implemented the option of allowing transfers out of TIAA.

This will restore each account to the 25% level, and you have nothing more to do for another year.

With the use of a hand calculator, this process should take no more than 30 minutes a year. This approach does require one very important personal quality—*self-discipline,* as it requires you to take action against the trends. At precisely the time you are reading in the newspapers and hearing talk at cocktail parties about how stocks are going down, your strategy tells you to invest more of your retirement money in stocks. This can be psychologically difficult to do. Moreover, if you are the type who gets frustrated because your investment strategy does not seem to produce quick results, forget this approach. If you can discipline yourself to stick with the strategy for the long pull, but you want to spend very little time on money matters, they may be just the approach for you.

Investor Selected Allocation Strategy

This strategy is exactly like the one just described except that instead of our funds receiving equal allocations, the allocations will be selected by the investor based on his or her own personal situation and investment objectives. It is not necessary to use four funds; either fewer or more might better meet a particular investor's needs.

We can look at several alternative applications of this strategy. There may be an ultra conservative investor who wants to take advantage of this approach but with minimal risk. An appropriate portfolio for that person might be:

40% to TIAA
20% to CREF Passive Equities Fund
20% to CREF Bond Fund
20% to CREF Balanced Fund

The portfolio is conservative in several ways. TIAA, the least volatile of the four funds used, comprises 40% of the total. Another 20% is in a bond fund, which will fluctuate in price as interest rates change, but should still be less volatile than the equities funds. Finally, the two equity funds should be the least volatile of the equity funds available.

An alternative to this approach which would still provide a conservative, low risk portfolio might be accomplished using only three funds:

40% to TIAA
30% to CREF Bond Fund
30% to CREF Passive Equities Fund

Another participant may have a higher risk tolerance and want a more aggressive portfolio, with more volatility. An appropriate mix of funds could be:

40% to CREF Actively Managed Fund
20% to CREF International Equities Fund
20% to CREF Bond Fund
20% to TIAA

Another alternative would be what might be called an *age related strategy*. This would involve an allocation that is designed to be adjusted and reduce risk about once a decade as the participant grows older. It would look something like the numbers shown in Figure 4.1. You can, of course, adjust the percentages to suit yourself and even use different funds if you prefer. All of the plans described would be implemented in the same two-step procedure—set the monthly allocations on the basis of the preferred percentages, and then once each year make the necessary adjustments in the accumulation balances to bring them back into line with those percentages.

Variable Allocation Strategies

Variable allocation strategies are similar to permanent allocation strategies, but they differ in two important ways. First, with variable allocation strategies, the percentage distribution for the monthly allocations and the accumulation balances need not be the same. Second, and this is why they are called *variable,* with variable allocation strategies the monthly allocations or accumulations may vary based on *external economic factors* rather than on the preferences of the investor.

This approach will involve somewhat more time than those described above. It will be necessary for the investor to set aside perhaps 15 minutes or so a week to check the markets and whatever economic indicators are being used.

The goal of variable allocation strategies is to be more heavily invested in the stock market (equity funds) when economic factors are favorable and mainly in other investments when conditions affecting the stock market are unfavorable. Such strategies often use interest rates as an

	Age 25	*Age 35*	*Age 45*	*Age 55*
CREF Actively Managed	40%	35%	25%	20%
CREF International Equities	30%	25%	10%	
CREF Bond Fund	20%	25%	25%	30%
CREF Money Market			15%	20%
TIAA	10%	15%	25%	30%

Figure 4.1. Percentages for Monthly Allocation and Accumulation Balances

indicator of when to be invested in equities on the assumption that equities usually move in an inverse relationship with interest rates.

Interest Rate Strategy

One such approach recommended by William E. Donoghue, who has probably done more research on money market funds than anyone else in the investment field. In his book, *No-Load Mutual Fund Guide,* he presents what he calls his "12 per cent solution." This involves switching between a money market fund and a stock fund based on the interest rate yield of money market funds, as follows:

Invested in Money Market Fund	Money Market Funds Yield	Invested in Equity Fund
100%	*13%*	*0%*
75%	*12%*	*25%*
50%	*11%*	*50%*
25%	*10%*	*75%*
0%	*9%*	*100%*

Donoghue says you should be 100% invested in money market funds if they are paying 13% or more. When the rates fall to 12% you should begin to move a portion of your funds into stock funds. Donoghue was writing in the early 1980's when interest rates were very high, and someone using his approach today might want to reduce all the numbers in the center column, perhaps by two or three points. Donoghue himself would likely recommend such an adjustment.

A TIAA-CREF participant could adjust the chart and implement a plan as follows:

Invested in Money Market Fund	Money Market Funds Yield	Invested in Equity Fund
80%	*10%*	*20%*
60%	*9%*	*40%*
40%	*8%*	*60%*
20%	*7%*	*80%*

We believe strongly in diversification and in the principle that one should not have all of his or her investment money in one place. Therefore, this chart does not use the 100% figure. It never has more than 80% in either the equity or the money market fund. An investment strategy using this chart could be implemented in the following way:

1. Choose an equity fund, perhaps the CREF Actively Managed Equity Fund, and use it in conjunction with the CREF Money Market Fund.
2. Set your monthly allocations so that 50% of your contributions go into each of the funds each month. *Then leave these allocations alone.* Don't attempt to adjust them each time you change your accumulation balances. To get started, let your funds accumulate 50% in each account until a change in money market yield calls for a change in the accumulation percentages.
3. Use a chart similar to the one above, or alter it to satisfy yourself. Based on this chart, you will be 80% invested in the CREF Money Market Fund whenever it is yielding more than 10% and only 20% invested in that fund when it is yielding less than 7%.
4. Once each week call TIAA-CREF (1–800–223–1290) and you will hear a recorded message which will tell you the current values of CREF funds and will also give you the current yield of the CREF Money Market Fund.
5. As the yield on the money market fund changes to the next significant "whole number," call TIAA-CREF (1–800–842–2252) and adjust your accumulations balances based on your chart. You will find that you will not be making frequent changes. Interest rates usually do not fluctuate so rapidly as to cause you to make more than one or two such transfers a year.

Why, you may ask, do we recommend shifting the accumulations balances but not the monthly allocations in this plan? We want to keep the plan simple to implement while protecting your retirement funds. Using this approach, the shift of accumulation balances will protect the money you have invested through the years from major loss while at the same time providing that the new money you are investing, your monthly allocations, will take advantage of the current price declines.

An advantage of this approach is its "do-it-yourself" nature. You can adjust the numbers in the chart and the frequency of adjustment to suit yourself. If you prefer to check with TIAA-CREF monthly rather than weekly, the plan will still work. Donoghue says his "12% solution" would have yielded an average compound rate of 19.1% in the years from 1975 (when money market funds were a very new idea) to the time of the publication of his book, a figure considerably above what would be expected from a "buy, hold and forget it" approach.

Trend Reversal Strategies

Martin Zweig suggests another way to use variable allocation strategies. Zweig is himself a former professor and has a Ph.D. in Finance from Michigan State University. He takes a very systematic, research oriented approach to his investment analysis. In his book, *Winning With New IRA's,* Zweig says a 4% reversal in direction is likely to indicate a major trend shift for stock and bond funds. Although it takes a little more time than the plane outlined above, this approach can be applied to TIAA-CREF funds.

Our variation of the 4% reversal strategy, as applied to TIAA-CREF funds, would be as follows. If a fund has moved gradually, week by week, to a price of $10 and then falls to $9.60, that would represent a 4% decline. It would then be time to sell the fund. The change need not occur all at once. If a fund reaches a price level of $10, then drops over several weeks to $9.90, $9.85, $9.75 and $9.60, when it reaches $9.60 that represents a 4% decline from the high. That would be the sell signal. The same principle would apply when prices start back up. When a fund rises 4% above its low, that becomes a buy signal.

You can use the trend reversal strategy in the following manner:

1. Choose two or three equity funds to use along with the CREF Money Market Fund. Using more than one equity fund lowers risk through diversification.
2. Choose a set of monthly allocation percentages so as to distribute your contributions rather evenly among the three funds. You might want to have 40% of your monthly contributions going into the most conservative of your three funds and 30% into each of the other two.
3. Once a week call TIAA-CREF (1–800–223–1290) and check the closing price of each of your equity funds. Keep a written record of the weekly closing prices of each fund so that you can identify when a 4% trend reversal has occurred.
4. When an equity fund falls 4%, shift the accumulation (but not the monthly allocation) into the CREF Money Market Fund. Our philosophy here is the same as for the interest rate strategy. Shifting the accumulation protects the money you have already invested. Leaving the monthly allocation alone enables your new money to take advantage of the current lower prices.
5. When an equity fund which has been falling in price reverses direction and rises 4%, shift a portion of the money in the Money Market Fund back into that fund. You will probably want to invest an amount in the fund which about equals the

amount you shifted out of that fund the last time you moved into the Money Market Fund.

Remember, so long as the price is moving in the same direction without a 4% price reversal, leave your investments alone. This way you will profit when the long term price trend of your equity funds is rising, and when the trend is downward, your money will be sitting safely in the Money Market Fund. Zweig says his 4% model (only slightly different from our approach) would have provided an average annual return of 18.9% if used between 1966 and 1985.

If you decide the 4% reversal approach causes you to make more switches that you like, you can adjust and use a 5%, 6% or other figure for your reversal number. This will cause you to make fewer switches, but it will also reduce your return somewhat as you catch each trend reversal somewhat later in the reversal process. This approach, like those above, has the advantage of allowing you to adjust it to meet your own needs and preferences.

Summary

Asset allocation strategies are based on the most fundamental principle of investing—diversification. They recognize that different types of investments do well at different times.

Permanent asset allocation strategies have the advantage of being easily understood and simple to implement. They also require very little time to monitor. Variable asset allocation strategies enable the investor to make adjustments in order to take advantage of changes in economic and financial conditions. They take somewhat more time to implement and monitor than permanent asset allocation strategies, but they are still easily maintained by an investor who wants to devote very little time to managing his or her investments.

Bibliography

Browne, Harry, *The Economic Time Bomb,* St. Martin's Press, 1989. Contains revised and updated material discussing the strategies he outlines in the book listed next.

Browne, Harry, *Why the Best-Laid Investment Plans Usually Go Wrong,* Morrow Press, 1987.

Donoghue, William E., with Thomas Tilling, *No-Load Mutual Fund Guide,* Harper and Row, 1983.

Merriman, Paul A., and Dowd, Merle E., *Market Timing with No-Load Mutual Funds,* Henry Holt and Co., 1986.

Zweig, Martin, *Winning with New IRA's,* Warner, 1987.

Chapter 5

Dollar Averaging Strategies

Participants in TIAA-CREF regularly make use of dollar averaging even though they may not realize they are doing so. Dollar averaging is the process of investing the same amount in a particular stock, mutual fund or other investment instrument at regular intervals. The result is that more of that investment instrument is purchased when prices are low than when prices are high. This illustrated in Figure 5.1

The investor here is investing $20 every month in the stock of ABC Company. We are assuming for purposes of the example that one may buy fractional shares, which in fact is the case with mutual funds or retirement funds such as TIAA-CREF. It is obvious that $20 purchases more when the price is low than when it is high. The investor's $20 bought 10 shares in March, when the price was $2 per share, but only 2.5 shares in June, when the price had risen to $8 a share.

We can see from the example that the average price of a share of stock over the six month period was $4.67. However, the process of dollar

$20 Monthly Investments

Month	Price of ABC Stock	Monthly Investment	Shares Purchased
January	$ 5	$20	4
February	4	20	5
March	2	20	10
April	4	20	5
May	5	20	4
June	8	20	2.5
Totals		$120	30.5

Average share price over six months—$4.67
Average cost of shares purchased—$3.93

Figure 5.1. Dollar Averaging Purchases of ABC Company Stock

averaging, i.e. buying more shares when the price is low, enabled the investor to buy his 30.5 shares at an average cost of only $3.93 per share.

Dollar averaging is automatically at work for TIAA-CREF participants. Their contributions, sent in monthly by their employer, are usually the same each month. They might change only once a year, when the employee gets a salary adjustment or perhaps changes jobs. Therefore, these equal monthly contributions will buy more of a CREF equity fund when the price is low than when it is high. Thus, the CREF investor who does nothing in the way of investment planning is nevertheless taking advantage of the principle of dollar averaging.

Dollar Averaging Philosophy

The principle of dollar averaging is based on two fundamental assumptions. The first is that the long term trend of the stock market is up. This has been true for the nearly two centuries since the New York Stock Exchange was founded in 1792. Through the twentieth century, when we have had rather accurate measures of stock market movement, the average annual rise in the market has been between 9 and 10%. This is very important to the concept of dollar averaging. One would obviously not want to invest month after month, year after year, in any investment instrument whose long term price trend is down. While the fact that the market has gone up in the past does not guarantee it will do so in the future, it is still a reasonable assumption on which to build an investment strategy.

The second assumption is that the price of any specific investment instrument will fluctuate. While the long term price trend may be up, the price will not move in a straight-line upwardly direction. There will be quite significant short term ups and downs in the price. One can expect that certain investments, such as the CREF International Equities Fund and the CREF Actively Managed Equities Fund, will be more volatile than others.

The price fluctuation is what allows dollar averaging to work. The price needs to go down sometimes as well as up so that more shares can be purchased at the lower prices.

If these two assumptions, that there will be short term price fluctuations but that the long term price trend of equities will rise, are correct, the investor can profit by using a strategy based on dollar averaging.

Using Dollar Averaging

As noted above, the principle of dollar averaging will automatically be at work for the TIAA-CREF investor. The active investor can, however, use a strategy that will make dollar averaging an even more powerful investment tool. Such a plan is described below.

While the plan may seem complicated at first, it really is not. The plan is based on the simple principle of increasing the percentage of the monthly contribution that goes into an equities fund as the price of that fund falls. Then as the price rises, the percentage of monthly contribution going into that fund is reduced. The plan would be implemented as follows:

1. Begin by selecting one of the CREF equities funds to invest in (you can use the strategy simultaneously with more than one fund if you desire). Then establish your monthly allocations at 50% in the equity fund and 50% in the CREF Money Market Fund. At the end of the first month, note the closing price of the equity fund and that becomes your first *base price*. The base price is used for one purpose—when the price of the equity fund falls at least 10% from the base price, you change your monthly allocations so that more of your money is going to buy the equity fund.

2. Once each month, call TIAA-CREF (1–800–223–1290) and record the latest closing price of the equity fund. Keep a permanent record of these monthly closing prices. Then do one of four things:

   a. if the closing price is above the current base price, set the new closing price as your new base price.
   Example: Last month the fund closed at $20.00. This month it closes at $20.50. Twenty dollars and fifty cents becomes your new base price.

   b. if the closing price has fallen to a level at least 10% below your base price, call TIAA-CREF (1–800–842–2252) and adjust your monthly allocations. Shift from the 50/50 allocation so that 60% now goes into the CREF equities fund and 40% into the money market fund. Make NO adjustment in your accumulations; only in the monthly allocations.
   Example: Your base price, which may have been set one month ago or many months ago, is $20.50. This month your fund falls to $18.30. Since any price below $18.45 (20.50 minus 2.05) represents a decline of more than 10% from the base price, call TIAA-CREF and adjust your allocations to 60% for the equity fund and 40% for the money market fund.

Note: In succeeding months, the fund price may decline even more or it may go back up slightly. Remember that you just leave the allocations at 60/40. You do not change the 60/40 allocations until the price returns to at least the base price, as explained in c.

c. if you have been allocating your money on a 60/40 basis, and the price of the equity fund rises to at least the base price, return your allocation figures to 50/50. At this point you will also have a new base price to record.

Example: For several months you have been allocating your money on a 60/40 basis. Your base price through these months has been $20.50. Now your fund has moved up in price and closes this month at $21.25. Call TIAA-CREF and adjust your monthly allocation percentages back to 50/50. Then record $21.25 as your new base price.

d. if your fund price stays the same or declines in price but does not reach a figure at least 10% below the current base price, do nothing. Also, if you have already adjusted the allocations to 60/40, and the fund price does not rise at least to the base price, do nothing.

Example: Your current base price is $20.50. The closing price of the fund for the current month is $19.10. This is above the figure of $18.45, which would represent a decline of 10% from the base price, so just do nothing.

Figure 5.2 shows one year of activities using this plan. The right hand column shows which of the steps outlined above are illustrated by that month's action. Most funds would not be this volatile, but we have exaggerated the price movements to illustrate the various steps taken in implementing the strategy.

You may want to keep a chart of this type for your own use. It is a good way to keep a record of the current month's closing price, the base price and the actions taken in regard to the monthly allocations. As you keep the record month-by-month, you will become familiar with the system and it will not seem complicated at all.

Month	Closing Price	Base Price	Base Price Less 10%	Monthly Allocations Equity/Money Mkt	Action Taken	Example of Plan Step *
January	$20.00	$20.00	$18.00	50/50	Allocations set	
February	20.50	20.50	18.45	50/50	Base price adjusted	a)
March	19.10	20.50	18.45	50/50	No action taken	d)
April	18.30	20.50	18.45	60/40	Allocations adjusted	b)
May	17.90	20.50	18.45	60/40	No action	d)
June	16.40	20.50	18.45	60/40	No action	d)
July	18.50	20.50	18.45	60/40	No action	d)
August	19.75	20.50	18.45	60/40	No action	d)
September	21.25	21.25	19.12	50/50	Alloc. & base adjusted	c)
October	22.00	22.00	19.80	50/50	Base price adjusted	a)
November	20.25	22.00	19.80	50/50	No action	d)
December	19.40	22.00	19.80	60/40	Allocation adjusted	b)

* Letters in right hand column indicate which of the steps (a through d) described above are illustrated by that month's action.

Figure 5.2. Implementing the Dollar Averaging Strategy

Dollar Averaging Alternatives

This plan can be modified in various ways. An investor with higher risk tolerance might set the original monthly allocations at 60% to an equity fund and 40% to the money market fund. Then when the price declines more than 10% below the base price, the allocations would be adjusted to 70% for the equity fund and 30% for the money market fund. The 60/40 allocations, rather than 50/50, become the figures to which the plan reverts when the closing price rises back to the level of the base price.

A more risk averse investor can begin with allocations of 40% for the equity fund and 60% for the money market fund, and then adjust to 50/50 when the price declines. With this approach, the low risk investor will never have more than 50% of the monthly contributions going into equity funds.

Combining Strategies

Dollar averaging strategies work through changes in the monthly allocations. They do not make changes in the accumulations. An investor might want to combine dollar averaging with one of the asset allocation strategies discussed in the prior chapter. For example, one could use a permanent allocation strategy. The dollar averaging strategy would be used throughout the year, and changes would be made in the monthly allocations when appropriate. Then, once a year, the accumulations could be adjusted back to percentages called for by the permanent allocation strategy being used.

There are other combinations that can be used. Dollar averaging would work well in combination with an age related allocation strategy, which would call for changing the percentage goals only once a decade or so. The possible strategies are limited only by the creative thinking of the investor.

Summary

Dollar averaging is based on the assumptions that the long term price trend of equity funds will be up but that they will not rise in a straight line manner. Rather, there will be fluctuations in price that will enable the dollar averaging investor to take advantage of buying more of the fund when the price declines. The investor can make this strategy work in an even more powerful manner by using the plan described above.

The dollar averaging approach can also be combined with asset allocation strategies if the investor so desires. These strategies can be implemented with relatively little time commitment on the part of the investor. They should enable the investor to increase his investment return with minimal increase in risk.

Bibliography

Boone, Louis E., and Kurtz, David L., *Contemporary Personal Finance,* Random House, 1985. Chapter 16 provides a thorough explanation of dollar averaging.

Graham, Benjamin, *The Intelligent Investor,* Harper and Row, 1973.

Lichello, Robert, *How To Make $1,000,000 in the Stock Market Automatically,* Signet, 1985. The author presents a formula which resembles a sophisticated form of dollar averaging although it involves selling as well as buying.

Willis, Clint, "Beyond Dollar-Cost Averaging," *Money,* July, 1988, pp. 105–09.

Chapter 6

Transferring Accumulations: CREF Stock—CREF Money Market Account

In August of 1987, two months before the stock market "crash", a faculty member at our university was so worried about what he thought were lofty stock prices that he made an allocation change to 100 percent TIAA. Thinking that he had moved all his money out of stocks, he was elated and felt rather smug when the stock market tumbled 503 points on October 19th. What he later found out was that the allocation change did not affect the money previously invested in his CREF stock account. He suffered the stock loss along with all the other CREF Stock holders. The change he made was to *future* allocations, not to his current investments.

The distinction between transferring funds, which is the focus of this chapter, and making allocation changes is so important to the subject of this chapter that we will again discuss the differences. Transferring funds refers to the movement of investment dollars that are *currently* part of your TIAA-CREF investment portfolio (for example, moving an accumulated $10,000 from your CREF Stock fund account to your CREF Money Market fund account). Making an allocation change refers to changing the distribution of *future* payments to TIAA-CREF. As an example, if you currently have 50% of your monthly allocation of new retirement funds going to TIAA and 50% going to CREF STock, an example of an allocation change would be to have 60% of new monthly payments going to TIAA and 40% going to CREF Stock. The important distinction is that allocation changes affect the investment of future retirement funds as they are initially invested, while transfers affect the resting place for retirement money that is already in your TIAA-CREF accounts.

What Can Be Transferred?

TIAA-CREF provides a number of transfer options. The focus of this chapter is the option to transfer (switch) accumulated money between the CREF Stock account (or the CREF Passive Equities account) and the CREF Money Market account. Other transfer options will be discussed in the following chapter.

TIAA-CREF allows you to transfer all the money in your CREF Stock or Money Market account, or you can make a partial transfer if you wish (a minimum of $1000 is required on partial transfers). Currently there are no restrictions on how many transfers you can make in each quarter. All transfers are effective at the *close* of the New York Stock Exchange if instructions are received before the market closes (This is 4:00 PM Eastern Time or 1:00 PM Pacific Time). No intra-day postings are made. This means that if you make a transfer early on a Monday morning and later that day the market drops (or rises) 100 points, your allocation change will experience the end-of-day reading, not the value of your account at the moment you made the telephone call. If transfer instructions are received after the New York Stock Exchange has closed, the transfer will be made effective at the end of the *next* business day. Transfers can be made using an automated system, or if you prefer, with the assistance of TIAA-CREF personnel. In chapter 8, *Using Investor Services,* we'll discuss the actual mechanics of making a transfer.

Should You Make Transfers?

The first question you should ask yourself is whether you should consider making any transfers at all. Literally millions of working men and women have participated in successful retirement programs of one kind or another over the years, without becoming personally involved in making transfers. In most cases, of course, retirement program participants have not had an option to make transfers between various investment vehicles. For those that had an option, many have chosen not to exercise it and feel comfortable with their decision. Why would anyone want to go to the trouble to make transfers within their retirement account?

Making properly timed transfers over a working lifetime offers the potential to significantly increase the total accumulation available at retirement. If one could increase the rate of return just a few percentage points per year, on average, over a long period of time, a large increase in the ending balance would result. Figure 6.1 shows how compounding at slightly higher rates for a fixed sum of dollars can greatly affect an ending sum.

Values of a Single $10,000 investment at Given Compound Rates for Years Shown

Investment Horizon (years)	8 percent	12 percent	16 percent	20 percent
5	$ 14,693	$ 17,623	$ 21,003	$ 24,883
10	21,589	31.058	44,114	61,917
15	31,722	54,736	92,655	154,070
20	46,610	96,463	194,461	383,380
25	68,485	170,000	408,740	953,660
30	100,630	299,600	858,500	2,273,800

Figure 6.1. The Effects of Higher Interest Rates on Ending Balances.

Let's say, for example, that you decide to actively manage just $10,000 of your retirement accumulations. If you compare the ending balance based on an 8 percent return to that of a 12 percent return, you can see a large difference. Over 30 years the balances would be $100,630 at the 8 percent rate and $299,600 at the 12 percent rate. Almost three times as much money from a four percent increase.

Other than attempting to increase the amount of money in your investment account, there are other reasons that you may want to establish a transfer program. One's retirement account not only has an important impact on an individual's life after retirement, but it can affect the participant during the working years as well. Relatively large accumulations of money make some people nervous, especially when the total value fluctuates. Therefore, psychological reasons as well as financial reasons are important considerations for implement a transfer program.

A buy and hold strategy (no transfers) guarantees a roller coaster ride for your CREF Stock accumulation balance. The stock market fluctuates, and it is not uncommon to see drops of 20 percent or more in the total value of a stock portfolio, one or two times each decade (this high-to-low change is termed the "drawdown" of the account). History has shown that the fluctuating stock market is riding on a long term up-trend, so the drops are not really all that important to a retirement-oriented investor with a long-term view. Over the short-term, however, these fluctuations can have a major psychological impact on holders of CREF Stock Units. Some participants watch their CREF Stock balance like a hawk, and have emotional difficulty handling a large drawdown from their account. A 20 percent drawdown, for example may be troubling for some investors to the point of disrupting mood and sleep patterns. For these individuals, a system that limits drawdowns by transferring money out of the volatile Stock fund when prices decline moderately is worthwhile, even if no additional monetary benefits accrue over the long term.

Another reason for developing a transfer system is to reduce the feeling of helplessness that many investors experience when accumulations are at the mercy of stock price movement. This feeling often arises when the stock market is at an all-time high and standard measures of stock valuation (for example, price-to-earnings ratios) indicate that the market is unrealistically overvalued and is therefore vulnerable to a setback (this was the situation in the Summer of 1987). Without the knowledge or ability to control CREF Stock accumulations, a participant may experience chronic worry and nervousness. An established transfer program with specific switching rules that tell the participant when to move in and out of the CREF stock market account provides an increased felling of control over one's destiny.

There are other factors involved in the decision to take charge of your funds by making transfers. Time is involved in all decision processes and developing a system for making transfers is not an exception. Unless you are willing to devote the time to self management, success will be difficult to achieve. Decisiveness is another requirement. When the decision to transfer funds is made, will you be able to do it? If "freezing up" occurs when the moment to take action arrives, the best of plans are worthless. Finally, an interest in managing your money is necessary. Without the natural interest, no long term program will be successful.

Basic Principles for a Successful Transfer Program

Principle 1: Transfer for Long-Term, Not Short-Term Gains

The stock market is extremely volatile over the short-term span of a few hours to a few days. It is very tempting to think that you may be able to "catch" every short-term rise and fall in stock prices, thereby amassing a large accumulation of money in a short period of time. In truth, no one has been able to do this consistently despite the heroic efforts of many hopeful speculators over decades. At present, the best model of short term market movements is noise or randomness, which defies prediction. A more realistic approach to take is to try to match your transfers with the major longer-term swings in the stock market instead of the short ones. Focus your efforts on movements that you expect to last for many months instead of a few weeks or less. These are the movements that will offer you the best opportunity to make profits.

Principle 2: Strive for Consistency

Allied with having a long term view is to have an orientation geared toward investment consistency. In investing, hitting a lot of singles over many years is better than hitting a few home runs and occasionally striking out. Figure 6.2 below illustrates the difference between these two approaches. As the figure shows, the consistent but unspectacular results provide a greater ending balance over the five year period than the dramatic but wider swinging performance.

	Year 1	Year 2	Year 3	Year 4	Year 5
Investor A	+ 12 %	+ 12 %	+ 12 %	+ 12 %	+ 12%
Investor B	+ 20%	− 50 %	+ 50 %	+ 50%	+ 15 %

Total Return for Each Dollar Invested: Investor A $1.84   Investor B $1.55

Figure 6.2 Consistent versus Variable Returns

Principle 3: Diversifying Your Investments

As we have repeatedly stated throughout this book, one of the best ways to reduce risk is to diversify your money across different types of investments. The old folk saying of not putting all your eggs in one basket is a common way of expressing this principle. A "what if" scenario can best illustrate the advantages of diversification. If a TIAA-CREF participant has an even 50-50 percent split of investment dollars between TIAA and CREF and if the stock market should suddenly drop by a sickening 30 percent, total retirement fund accumulations would only be reduced by 15 percent. Moreover, if you had half of your CREF funds in the CREF Money Market account at the time of the stock market sell off, then the total reduction in accumulated value would be only 7.5 percent, hardly enough of a decline to cause even a single hair on your head to turn white. By making use of several different investment vehicles, overall loss is minimized should a disaster befall any one of them.

Principle 4: Make Incremental Transfers

If you are fortunate enough to have a working crystal ball, we recommend transferring all of your CREF stock accumulations when the crystal gives you buy and sell signals. If, for example, you knew for certain that stocks would double in value next year, then you would be foolish not to put all of your money into stocks. You also might want to borrow money and even sell your house to raise money to invest in the stock market.

For those of us who must make financial decisions without the benefit of a perfect source of information, an all-or-nothing approach makes little sense. A realistic model of the financial markets and of the world in general should make use of probabilities. An incremental approach to making transfers requires money to be moved in portions rather than all at once. This method allows you to adjust your stock exposure in approximate proportion with the degree of certainty and uncertainty you have toward the future direction of stock prices.

Principle 5: Keep It Simple

Most TIAA-CREF participants have years ahead of them before retirement, many have decades. Unless your financial management system is straightforward, it will sooner or later be neglected. The methods we discuss in this chapter attempt to be simple in their understanding and execution. The economic evidence approach that we first discuss only requires weekly monitoring of a few key indicators. The model building approach, discussed later, requires a bit more effort, but still can be understood by anyone. As we will see, the use of a personal computer reduces the computation time to a negligible amount, making even model building easy.

The Economic Evidence Approach

The idea behind this approach to making transfers is to adjust exposure to stocks (CREF stock account or CREF Passive Equities account) based on economic risk as defined by a few specific indicators. The method requires you to keep your CREF Stock portion fully invested when economic risk is low. As the risk increases, transfers are made out of the stock fund into the haven of the CREF Money Market account where your money earns the prevailing interest rate with no risk. As the risk factors return to normal, transfers are made back to the CREF Stock account(s).

This method attempts to find economic evidence that can be used as "warning flags" of possible trouble for the stock market. While there are many factors that act as concurrent barometers of the economy's health, (GNP growth, company profits, budget deficit, value of the U.S. dollar, inflation rate, employment rate, and so on), they have historically been of little value for indicating when to get into and out of stocks. What can be used to provide advance warning of possible trouble for stocks? Two types of evidence have met the test of time and will be discussed in this chapter; interest rate trends and the trend of stock prices themselves.

Warning Flag I: Increasing Interest Rates

Why are rising interest rates one of the most reliable warning flags for indicating the increased risk of holding stocks? First, rising interest rates change investor's perceptions concerning the future attractiveness of competing types of investments. As an example, if we consider that the long-term average return from stocks is about 9 percent, when money market funds rise to near this level, investors can obtain stock-class returns without the risk of owning stocks. Money market funds therefore become stiff competition for investment dollars when compared to the stock market. New investment dollars that would ordinarily flow into stocks may be diverted into the no-risk high yielding alternative. The reduction in demand for stocks can act as a brake to rising prices and may contribute to a general decline. A downward movement of stock prices can happen when investors actually sell stock to obtain the high risk-free return.

Another reason to be wary of rising interest rates is that corporate profits eventually suffer if rates rise high enough. Most corporations make use of debt financing to one degree or another. As interest rates rise, the cost of raising money through the use of debt also rises. This is a cost of doing business, and like any other cost, it reduces the level of profits, making the company less attractive as an investment.

Rising interest rates also affect the *demand* side of the business equation. As rates rise, the number of people that can afford home mortgages falls. This translates into fewer new home sales which has a rippling effect through the economy as building supplies, construction labor, durable goods (washers, refrigerators, etc.) are also affected in a negative way. Automobiles are another item that typically require a loan for purchase. Again, higher rates means higher monthly payments which in turn means fewer auto purchases. This effect is not only concentrated on big ticket items. Many consumers use credit cards. As interest rates rise, the cost of carrying the credit balance also goes up, making it more difficult to purchase additional goods.

Rising interest rates also affect investors with margin investment accounts, as the broker loan rate goes up along with the general interest rate increase. This means that stock investors must obtain a higher rate of return on margined investments, just to break even. During these times, investors on margin tend to be more cautious, resulting in a reduction in the demand for stocks.

In summary, the old stock market saw, "don't fight the interest rate trend" is important for the market timer to keep in mind. When interest rates rise it is a time of increased economic and stock-market risk, so the timer should be prepared to "lighten the load" by transferring money from CREF stock to the CREF money market account.

Warning Flag II: A Downward Trend in Stock Prices

Trends in stock prices tend to persist. If you can recognize the major movement in stock prices, you can take advantage of the trend by "going with the flow". When prices are generally rising you can own stocks and thereby enjoy the ride up. When they are falling you can get out to avoid a future loss, and get back in at a lower level when they began rising again.

Major trends can last for some time, with falling prices often begetting more falling prices as "crowd psychology" takes over. Some major falling stock trends have lasted from months to years, with recent examples in 1961–1962, 1966, 1969–1970, 1973–1974, 1981–1982, and 1984.

For both stock price movement trends and interest rate trends, the practical problem for the market timer is to develop a procedure to determine major movements while avoiding the minor but frequent "jiggles". A major objective of the following section is to aid you in this process.

Setting Up a Program for Transferring from CREF Stock Account to CREF Money Market Account

As we previously mentioned, if an indicator could be found that works 100 percent of the time, i.e., tells you to sell when the market reaches its peak and tells you when to re-buy when it hits the bottom of every major move, then you should make all your decisions based on the reading of that one indicator. Unfortunately, no one has yet discovered such an indicator. Until one is discovered, a probabilistic approach, rather than a deterministic one, is more appropriate and will therefore be discussed here.

Your first step in setting up a transfer program is to find and continually monitor a small group of indicators that have a good historical track record and that make theoretical sense. They have to give unambiguous signals so there is no doubt when a transfer signal is given. As we stated previously, three or four of these indicators should be used so money will be incrementally moved, thereby minimizing the negative effects of a bad signal. For those TIAA-CREF participants who think that they can intuitively know when to transfer their money, we would suggest that intuition be treated as just another indicator, thereby increasing by one the number of indicators you use for making your transfers. History has shown that using intuition *exclusively* for buying and selling securities is a prescription for very poor long-term performance.

Many stock market timers leave a residual amount (20–25%) in their stock account that is not made a part of their transfer program. This "not to be transferred" portion recognizes the fact that it is difficult for any indicator or group of indicators to find the exact top or bottom of stock market movements. Moreover, the market has a history of making new recovery highs from major declines anyway, if given enough time.

Interest Rate Based Indicators

Interest Rate Indicator 1: Federal Reserve Activity

Activities of the Federal Reserve Board have been an excellent indicator of the future long-term direction of stock prices. The rules for using their activity as an indicator are follows:

Sell signal: When the Federal Reserve raises the discount rate for the third time in a row after at least one decrease.

Buy signal: When the discount rate has been dropped for the second time in a row after at least one increase.

These rules attempt to define "tight money" and "loose money" time periods. Past stock-price behavior has shown that when money is tight and expensive, stocks are at risk. When interest rates are dropping, the environment for stocks is more favorable. Figure 6.3 indicates just how this indicator has worked in the past.

	S & P 500 6 months Later	S & P 500 1 year Later
Second Decrease	+16.1%	+30.5%
Third Increase	−1.1%	−5.0%

Source: *Encyclopedia of Technical Market Indicators* by Robert W. Colby and Thomas A. Meyers

Figure 6.3. Federal Reserve Actions and Stock Market Performance.

Interest Rate Indicator 2: The Yield Curve

A second indicator of market risk based on interest rates is the current shape of the "yield curve". The yield curve represents the relationship between long-term and short-term interest rates. If we think of an interest rate as being the cost of renting money, then it should be expected that short-term interest rates would be lower than long-term interest rates. If you put yourself in place of the lender of the money then it is easy to understand why. If you are going to lend someone money for thirty years, you would want an interest rate payment that not only seems reasonable currently, but also has an extra amount built into the rate to cover possible economic uncertainties that may take place over the next thirty years. If, for example, inflation should go up significantly over the years, the principal and interest payments that you receive from the borrower would be worth less to you in terms of actual purchasing power.

If you were lending money to someone for the next three months, however, the uncertainty would not be much of a worry to you, since you will be getting your money back soon. Normally, therefore, long-term interest rates are higher than short-term interest rates. If interest rates were plotted on a graph, the normal relationship would be as shown in figure 6.4.

There are times when the yield curve "inverts". During this time short-term rates actually exceed long-term rates. Figure 6.5 illustrates this type of curve, which is downward sloping.

This downward sloping yield curve arises from actions of the Federal Reserve Board. Short-term rates are increased higher than long rates in a conscious effort to slow down the pace of economic activity. This typically happens when inflation is increasing to a point where the Federal Reserve thinks it may get out of hand and start an uncontrolled upward spiral. Inverting the yield curve is one way of stopping runaway inflation before it starts.

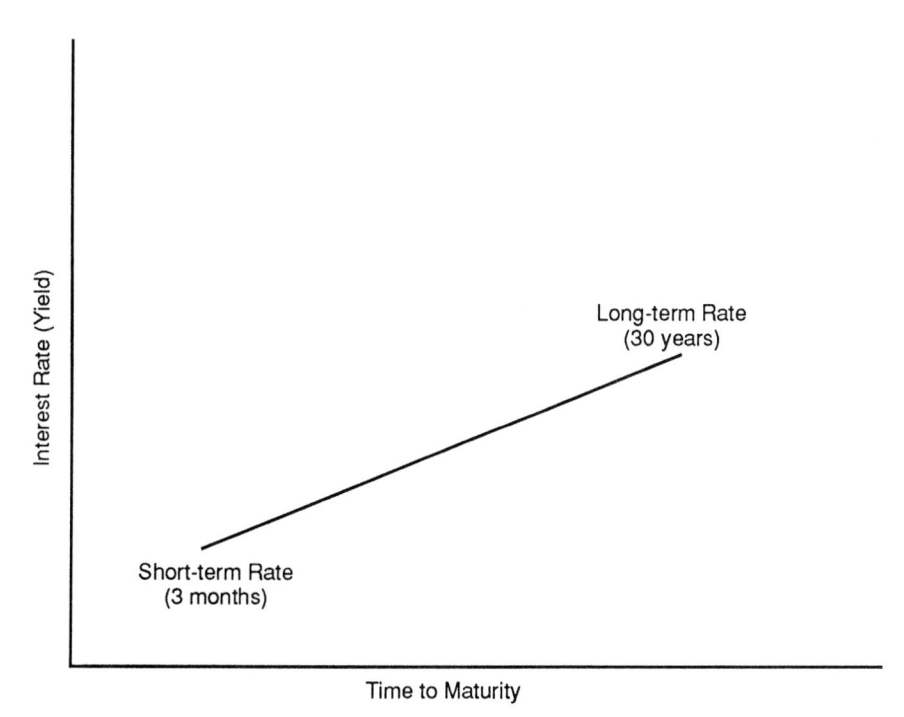

Figure 6.4. A "Normal" Yield Curve

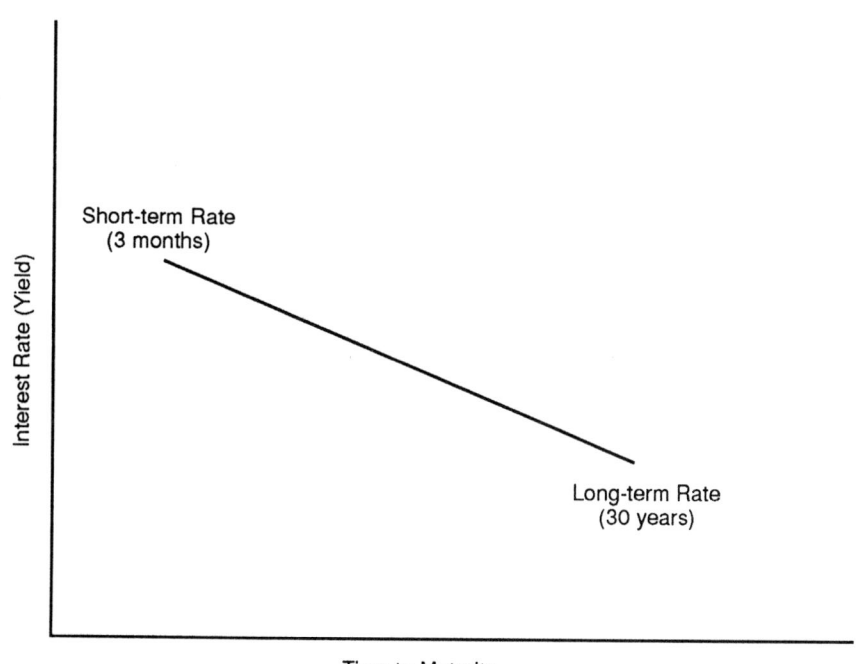

Figure 6.5. An "Inverted" Yield Curve

It is interesting to note that every recession that has occurred since World War II was preceded by an inverting of the yield curve. Every inversion of the yield curve, however, did not result in a recession (it happened about eighty percent of the time). The record of the yield curve and its effect on the stock market is represented by the S&P 500 average is shown in figure 6.6.

To use this indicator it is only necessary to look in the Wall Street Journal in the "Credit Markets" section. There you will see the current picture of the yield curve. If the 3 months rate has moved higher than the 30 year rate on the maturities scale, then the curve has inverted and a sell signal is given. When the 3 month rate drops down below the 30 year rate, then a buy signal is given. To prevent possible short term "whipsaws" in the indicator, we recommend that any inversion in the curve that occurs during the week maintain its position until the end of the week for it to be registered as valid. Put another way, use only weekly monitoring of the

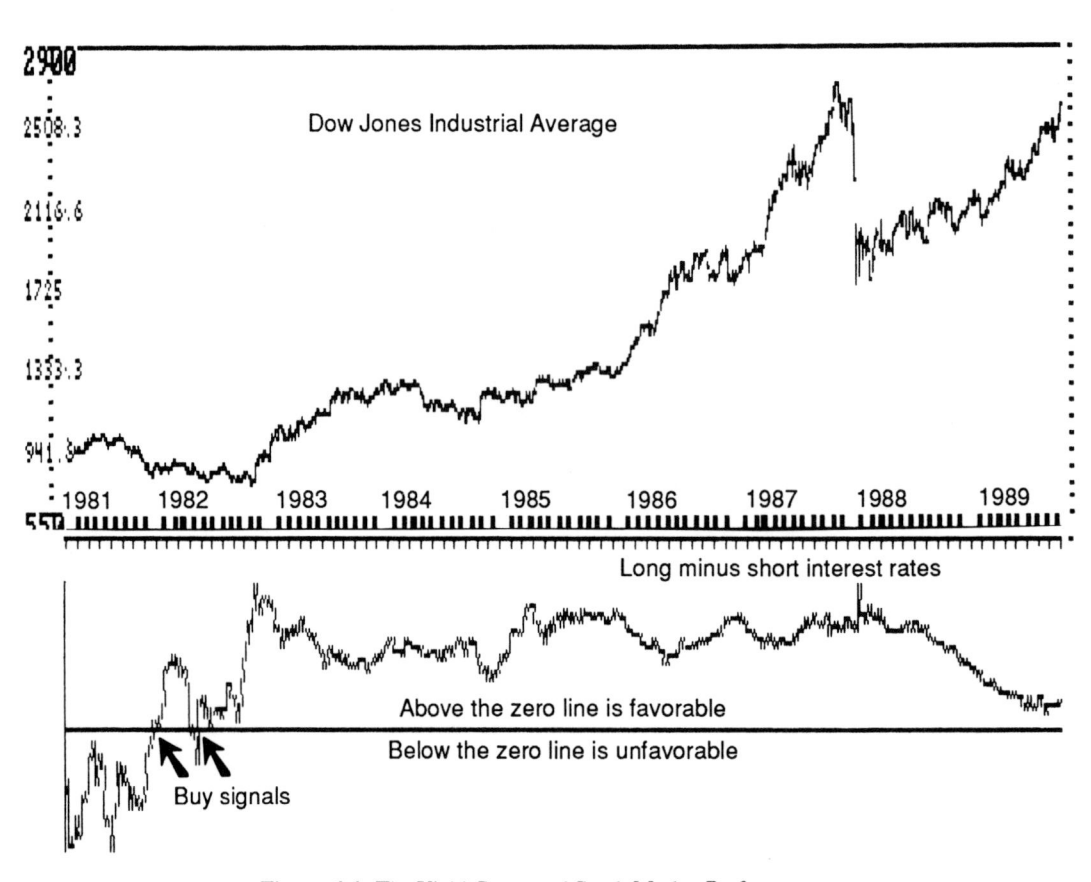

Figure 6.6. The Yield Curve and Stock Market Performance

yield curve rather than daily monitoring. This will prevent you from having quick intra-week reversals that would require you to sell and re-buy over an extremely short period of time.

Price Movement Indicators

Price Movement Indicator 1: Trend of the S&P 500 Index with Confirmation

This indicator makes use of the Standard and Poor's 500 index of large companies to define the trend of the overall market. If the S & P 500 has been rising but reverses to the downside by a significant amount, and this is confirmed by a downtrend in the Transportation average, then a sell signal is given. You would then proceed to transfer money from the CREF Stock to the CREF Money Market account. If the opposite condition occurs; a significant reversal to the upside from a prolonged decline, then a buy signal is given if confirmation occurs from the Transportation Average.

This approach assumes that the CREF stock portfolio movement is highly correlated with the movement of the general stock market. Since the CREF stock account is well over 50 percent indexed to the Standard and Poor's 500 Index, this assumption is generally valid. Moreover, the fund is so large (over 30 billion in assets) it almost *is* the market. When the proposed CREF Indexed Portfolio becomes available, a greater correlation with the S & P 500 may be observed. Figure 6.7 shows the composition of the CREF Stock account as of January 1, 1989 and it also provides a comparison of the CREF stock account to the general market. As can be seen, the fluctuations are quite similar.

An easy way to find transfer signals for this system is to look in *Investor's Daily* newspaper. Each day the newspaper shows a chart of the S & P 500 index with its 200 day moving average, and on Tuesday and on Thursday the Transportation Average is shown with its 200 day moving average.

The 200 day moving average for the S & P 500 represents the "anchor" for determining if the market's trend is up or down. As long as the S & P 500 is above its average of the last 200 days (the moving average line), the trend of prices is defined as up. If its value drops below its average value of the past 200 days, its trend is defined as down.

The defined trend reversals, however, are only tentative CREF Stock to CREF Money Market transfer signals. To get an actual sell or buy signal, a confirmation must be obtained from the Transportation average. The

CREF-STOCK COMPOSITION

Total Percentage of Market Value in Terms of Security Tape

S & P Index Securities	Non—S & P Indexed Securities	Selected Domestic Securities	Foreign Securities	Other
59.7%	9.1%	17.6%	11.5%	2.1%

CREF-STOCK PERFORMANCE

Average Annual Compound Rates of Total Return:		S & P 500 Index	CREF-Stock Annuities
1 YEAR	(1/1/88 to 12/31/88)	16.72%	17.46%
3 YEARS	(1/1/86 to 12/31/88)	45.18%	50.42%
5 YEARS	(1/1/84 to 12/31/88)	103.18%	108.94%
10 YEARS	(1/1/79 to 12/31/88)	349.42%	360.19%

Source: *College Retirement Equities Fund Prospectus. April 1, 1989.*

Figure 6.7. CREF-Stock: Composition and Performance.

same method for defining a trend is used on this average; its position with respect to the 200 day moving average. If the current value is below the moving average it represents a downtrend, if up, an uptrend. Figure 6.8 graph shows how this system works.

Price Movement Indicator 2: The Advance-Decline Line

Another way to gauge the general movement of the stock market is to look at the *number* of stocks that are going up and down, instead of the current value of stock prices. This is a useful alternative approach because a divergence in movement of an index from the overall market can occur from takeovers or arbitrage efforts in a limited number of high-capitalization stocks. When this happens, looking at prices alone can be deceptive, as they may not reflect the health of the overall market.

The advance-decline indicator attempts to track the pulse of the broad market. It is developed from the cumulative difference between weekly advancing and declining stocks on the New York Stock Exchange. The indicator requires about fifteen minutes of effort each week to update and as-

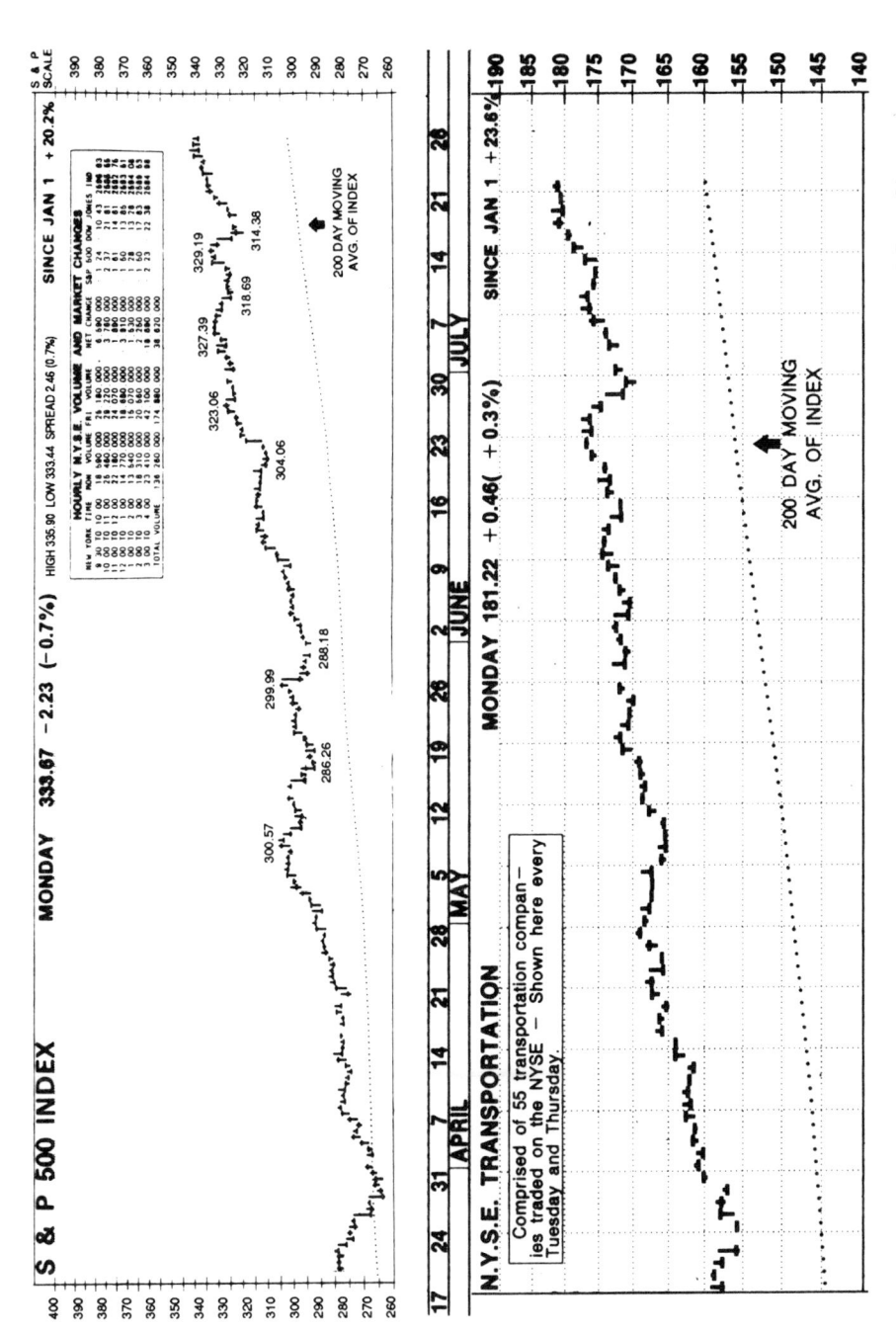

Figure 6.8. *Investor's Daily* Graphs for Definition of Major Trend. Reprinted by permission of INVESTOR'S DAILY, America's Business Newspaper. (July, 24, 1989), © INVESTOR'S DAILY, INC., 1989.

MARKET ADVANCE/DECLINE TOTALS

Weekly Composite	NYSE
Total Issues	2150
Advances	1150
Declines	1000

Figure 6.9. Advance—Decline Data

sess its status. Data can be obtained from the Sunday editions of most large city newspapers, and other sources such as *Barron's*. Figure 6.9 shows an example of what the data looks like.

To create the basic data set to make the indicator work, it is necessary to subtract the weekly declines on the New York Stock Exchange from the weekly advances. The resultant number is added (or subtracted if it is a negative number) from a running total of the data. Each week's new number is appended to the existing data set. To make the weekly computations easier, an initially large number (for example, 20,000) is used to start the process going, and insure an easier-to-work-with positive cumulative total.

If we look at the advance-decline data from the example shown in figure 6.9, the difference is 1150 – 1000 = 150. This number is added to 20,000 to yield 20,150 for the first week. If the second week's difference was 300, the cumulative total would then be 20,450. In some weeks there will be more down stocks than up stocks. In these cases the numeric difference will be negative. For example, if there were 700 up stocks in a given week and 900 down stocks, the difference would be –200. If this happened in the third week of our hypothetical example, the cumulative total for that week would be 20,450 – 200, or 20,250.

The cumulative totals create what is known as the weekly advance-decline line for the New York Stock Exchange. This process continues each week, creating a new cumulative total which is appended to the previous data set. As the weeks go by a larger and larger data set is created.

In order to determine discrete buy and sell signals, down trends and uptrends in the cumulative advances-declines have to be defined. This is accomplished by comparing the advance-decline line with its 10 week moving average. To find the moving average value it is simply necessary to take the current value and add it to the previous nine values, then divide by ten. This procedure is done each week. As long as the current advance-decline value is greater than its 10 week moving average value, the CREF Stock fund is held. When it becomes smaller, the signal is given to transfer funds to the safe haven of the CREF Money Market Fund. Figure 6.10 shows how the mathematics works for a hypothetical 15 week period.

There is independent evidence to show that this type of timing is successful in generating greater returns than a simple buy and hold approach. Eugene D. Veilleux in his book, *How to Switch Your Money Market fund for Maximum Profit* (E. D. Veilleux, 1983), used this method to time a number of commission free (no-load) stock mutual funds. He found an approximate doubling of returns from this strategy over a buy and hold approach. During the time period tested, approximately 5 signals were given on average each year.

When major up-movements occur in the stock market, substantial gains accrue because stock positions are maintained. When the market declines take place over a prolonged period, losses are minimized because the system will provide a transfer signal to the CREF money market account. When the market goes sideways, however, whipsaws occur, with small losses accruing. Despite the "false signals" given during sideways markets, this method is very forgiving since TIAA-CREF charges nothing to make a transfer. If a significant charge were made (as an investor ex-

BASE = 20,000

Week	Advances	Declines	Difference	Accumulation	10 week moving Average
1	1150	1000	+150	20,150	—
2	1200	980	+220	20,370	—
3	1100	1000	+100	20,470	—
4	900	1020	−120	20,350	—
5	1400	650	+750	21,100	—
6	1210	940	+270	21,377	—
7	1000	1050	−50	21,320	—
8	1100	922	+178	21,498	—
9	1400	620	+780	22,278	—
10	920	1150	−230	22,048	21,095.4*
11	810	1200	−390	21,658	21,240.2
12	960	1020	−60	21,598	21.305.0
13	740	1320	−580	21,018	21,414.8
14	1300	750	+550	21,568	21,526.6
15	1350	700	+650	22,218	21,638.4

*Sample calculation (average of ten week's accumulation):
(20,150 + 20,370 + 20,470 + 20,350 + 21,100 + 21,377 + 21,320 + 21,498 + 22,278 + 22,048)/10 = 21,095

Figure 6.10. Calculations for Advance-Decline Indicator

periences when buying or selling shares of stock through a stockbroker), economic benefits from this approach would be minimized.

Besides the four timing indicators just explained, there are numerous other possibilities for determining when to make a transfer. For an excellent summary of timing techniques, the book, *The Encyclopedia of Technical Market Indicators* by Robert W. Colby and Thomas A. Meyers (Dow Jones-Irwin, 1988) is recommended reading. Another source for the do-it-yourself timer is the "Psychological Indicators" section of the *Investor's Daily* newspaper. This section provides the current readings of a number of indicators whose value has been related in the past to stock market movement. Figure 6.11 provides an example of what this block of indicators looks like. Note that high and low values are provided for each indicator. This data is useful in setting parameters for generating buy and sell signals.

The Model Building Approach

A second way to obtain advice for timing the transfer of funds from the CREF STock amount to the CREF Money Market Account (and vice versa) is to use multi-factor mathematical models. These models can be constructed by yourself or you can make use of some ready made models. In either case, we believe the best approach is to incrementally switch; transfer *part* of your investment money when a signal is given, not all of it. It is fortunate that there are many models readily available for your use, or to customize to meet your needs.

Model I: The Wall Street Week Elves model

The Wall Street Week program airs every Friday evening on Public Television. This program, hosted by Louis Rukeyser, reviews the previous week's stock market activity and, with a group of knowledgeable panelists, discusses future directions for the stock market and the economy. While this is useful in its own right, the program also gives the current reading of the Wall Street Week Elves indicator, probably the most well known of all multifactor stock market timing models. (The current value of this model is also given in *Investors Daily* in the Psychological Indicators section. See figure 6.11).

This timing model was created by Robert Nurock, a frequent panelist on the show and president of Investor's Analysis, Inc. (P.O. Box 988, Paoli, PA 19301). The model is composed of ten different individual technical indicators, with the current status of each of these indicators given a value of plus one or minus one, depending whether each is forecasting

PSYCHOLOGICAL MARKET INDICATORS	Current	5 Year High	5 Year Date	5 Year Low	5 Year Date	12 Month High	12 Month Date	12 Month Low	12 Month Date
1. %Investment Advisors Bearish (50% = Bullish; 20% = Bearish)	33.9%	55.3%	(12/5/88)	10.6%	(4/1/86)	55.5%	(12/5/88)	26.1%	(6/12/89)
% Invest. Advisors Bullish (35% Bullish; 55% Bearish), - Investor's Intelligence	40.5%	68.3%	(4/4/86)	21.1%	(12/5/88)	46.5%	(5/29/89)	21.1%	(12/5/88)
2. Wall Street Week Index By R. Nurock (5 & more Bullish; - 5 & less Bearish)	0	+8	(11/6/87)	-5	(2/23/89)	+3	(8/26/88)	-5	(2/23/89)
3. Odd Lot Short Sales/Odd Lot Sales	0.69%	36.1%	(9/15/86)	0.04%	(9/11/87)	29.5%	(7/14/89)	0.19%	(10/11/88)
4. Public/NYSE Specialist Short Sales (above 0.6 Bullish; below 0.35 Bearish)	0.89	1.23	(5/13/88)	0.31	(10/23/87)	11.22	(8/12/88)	0.62	(6/2/89)
5. Short Interest Ratio (NYSE Short Interest/Avg Daily Volume prior 30 days)	2.97	3.86	(12/30/88)	1.67	(2/17/87)	3.86	(12/30/88)	2.57	(7/25/88)
6. Ratio of price premiums on Puts versus Calls	0.66	1.60	(2/17/87)	0.03	(10/19/87)	1.01	(1/31/89)	0.33	(11/16/88)
7. Ratio of Trading Volume in PUts versus Calls	0.51	0.96	(12/3/87)	0.26	(10/21/87)	0.74	(11/16/88)	0.30	(4/5/89)
8. Mutual Fund Share Purchases/Redemptions (X - Money Market Funds)	1.25	4.63	(10/1/85)	0.63	(10/30/87)	1.25	(5/31/89)	0.81	(8/1/88)
9. AMEX Daily Trading Volume as % of NYSE Daily Volume	8.43%	20.0%	(4/12/85)	2.56%	(6/17/88)	15.1%	(12/1/88)	4.18%	(10/27/88)
10. OTC Daily Trading Volume as % of NYSE Daily Volume	79.3%	143%	(5/20/88)	35.6%	(12/9/87)	136%	(7/22/88)	45.0%	(7/25/88)
11. Number of Stock Splits in INVESTORS DAILY INDEX (prior 30 days)	80	211	(6/26/86)	34	(3/3/88)	112	(7/3/89)	39	(11/18/89)
12. New Issues in Last Year as % of All Stocks on NYSE	1.29%	4.95%	(3/5/87)	1.29%	(7/24/89)	1.89%	(7/21/88)	1.29%	(7/24/89)
13. Price-to-Book Value of Dow Jones Industrial Average	2.48	4.37	(8/25/87)	1.13	(7/24/84)	2.56	(6/8/89)	2.10	(8/22/88)
14. Price to Earnings Ratio of Down Jones Industrial Average	11.2	21.0	(10/6/87)	9.79	(11/16/88)	11.3	(7/19/89)	9.79	(11/16/88)
15. Current Dividend Yield of Dow Jones Industrial Average	3.27%	5.05%	(7/24/84)	2.58%	(8/25/87)	3.80%	(11/16/88)	3.23%	(5/22/89)

Reprinted by permission of *Investor's Daily*, America's Business Newspaper, (July 24, 1989), *Investor's Daily, Inc.* 1989.

Figure 6.11. *Investor's Daily*, Psychological Market Indicators. Reprinted by permission of INVESTOR'S DAILY, America's Business Newspaper, (July 24, 1989), © INVESTOR'S DAILY, Inc., 1989.

higher or lower stock prices. When the aggregate sum of the ten indicators reaches plus 5, a buy signal is given. When it reaches minus five, a sell signal is given. The purpose of the model is to predict longer-term movements in the market (3 to 6 months and longer) not short-term swings.

While the Wall Street Week model has not been perfect, it has nevertheless provided good signals on long-term stock market movements. Colby and Meyers, in their book, *The Encyclopedia of Technical Market Indicators,* (Dow Jones-Irwin, 1988) report that for the 12 1/4 year period from October 18, 1974 to December 31, 1986 the Index correctly forecast the Dow Jones Industrial Average 70.4% of the time 13 weeks in advance, 79.5 percent of the time 26 weeks in advance, and 81.6 percent of the time 52 weeks in advance. Because its current value is provided on public television each week and in *Investor's Daily,* access to obtaining its current value is easy. For a complete discussion of The Wall Street Week Index performance record, including a chart showing actual buy and sell points, see the Colby and Meyers book (pages 548 to 554), previously mentioned.

Model II: The Zweig IRA stock timing model

Martin Zweig, in his book, *Winning with your IRA* (Warner, 1987) provides a simple two-factor stock market timing model for transferring money between stocks and money market funds (equivalent to CREF stock to CREF money market account transfers). Essentially, stocks are held only when two conditions are met: 1) interest rates are declining as measured by a declining prime rate, and 2) stock prices are rising as measured by a 4 percent or move upmove from the last bottom in prices. When both these conditions are met, stocks are held, otherwise, money is kept in a safe money market fund. Zweig shows all buy and sell signals given by this model since 1965 (see pages 140–141) in his book). The book also provides clear construction rules for maintaining this model over time. Zweig claims a return of 12.6 percent a year from the model as compared with the S&P 500 average annual performance of 9.1 percent. At first thought this may not seem like much but remember what we said previously, that just an additional few percent over a long period of time has a dramatic effect on an ending balance (see figure 6.1).

To make use of this model it is necessary to keep tuned to prime rate changes (*The Wall Street Journal* and all large city newspapers report these changes). To determine the four percent price change requires a mathematical calculation of four percent from the last high point (if the market is currently heading up). When the market average crosses the calculated value, a signal is given. See Zweig's book for more information and examples on making the required calculations.

Model III: The Stoken Strategic Climate Model

Richard Stoken, in his book, *Strategic Investment Timing* explains a multi-factor system that has identified major turns in the stock market within, on average, 4 percent of market tops and bottoms. Since 1931 the system has provided just 12 buy signals and 11 sell signals, so it doesn't require a lot of transfers. The system works by first categorizing the investment climate as favorable or hostile. This is accomplished through the identification of favorable and unfavorable interest rate periods, and favorable and unfavorable periods in the political cycle. Secondly, a stock market "buy" zone or "caution" zone is established by comparing the present position of the Dow Jones Industrial average with its past two year, and five year, high and low levels. Based on this information, buy and sell rules are generated and indicate when to move money into and out of stocks.

For specifics on the definitions of investment climate and market zones, as well as graphs which show all buy and sell signals, see the book *Strategic Investment Timing*, by Dick Stoken (Macmillan, 1984). An excellent summary of Stoken's rules and a summary of results can be found in the book, *Don't Sell Stocks on Monday"* by Yale Hirsch (Facts on File Publications, 1986).

Building Your Own Market Timing Model

Many stock market investors receive enjoyment from building their own unique long-term multi-factor timing model. If you choose to do so, the previously mentioned approaches represent a good starting point for proceeding. Certainly the level and direction of interest rates are factors that you should seriously consider incorporating into your model. The current direction that the market is moving is another. Whatever factors you choose, it is important to create unambiguous rules for combining the individual factors chosen, so you will know precisely when to take action. Once you make a model, it should be back-tested to discover how it worked in the past. It should not be too sensitive, so an excessive amount of switching will not take place. The model should be kept relatively simple so it can be easily kept up and faith can be maintained in it. It is also important not to be too naive in thinking that it (or any) model will provide perfect results. We live in a probabilistic world, and all models are in the final analysis simply attempting to put the odds in your favor. Finally, the development of a timing system must be viewed as a dynamic effort, so improvements are always possible. The proper management of retirement funds should be viewed as a life-long quest.

A computer and technical analysis software can be of great benefit to the model maker. Major tasks can be simplified, including the downloading of data from an information utility database and the manipulation of the data in various ways. As an example, the Dow Jones Market Analyzer PLUS software package (Dow Jones and Company, Princeton, N.J.) can be used to provide access to the Dow Jones News Retrieval Service and provide an ease of manipulation for financial data. Figure 6.12 illustrates some of the tasks that software of this type can accomplish.

Other financial software of value to the model-maker includes: Trendline II (Standard and Poor's Corp., 25 Broadway, New York, NY

Technical Market Indicators

    Simple moving average
    Weighted moving average
    Exponential moving average
    Modification of moving averages
    Support and resistance lines
    Trendlines
    Speed-resistance lines
    Linear least-squares fit line
    Modified least squares fit line
    Volume indicator charts
    User defined formulas

Data Retrieval

    Daily quotes (stocks, bonds, mutual funds)
    Historical daily price data
    Corporate descriptive information
    Economic descriptive information
    Historical articles from magazines and newspapers

Other functions

    Graphical support for all indicators
    Automated data access
    Automated charting
    Data editing
    Manual data entry
    Portfolio record keeping
    Portfolio report generation
    Daily quote reports

Figure 6.12. Dow Jones Market Analyzer Plus Software

10004); the Telescan analyzer (Telescan, Inc., 11011 Richmond ave., Suite 600, Houston, TX 77042); Compu-Track (Compu-Track Corp., 1021 9th st., New Orleans, LA. 70115) and Stock Analyzer (N-Squared Computing, 5318 Forest Ridge Rd., Silverton, OR 97381). Demonstration disks and printed literature are available for these software products. Financial publications such as *Barron's, Investor's Daily, Financial World* and others often have advertisements for additional financial software products suitable for generating market timing signals.

Purchasing Stock Market Timing Information

Some TIAA-CREF participants would like to have a system for making transfers, but do not have the time or interest to do it themselves. For these people, there are newsletters available that provide advice on when to move money between stock funds (like CREF stock) and Money market funds (like the CREF money account). The following are some to consider. Of course many others exist and can be found by reading advertisements in financial publications such as *Barron's, Investors Daily.,* and *Bull and Bear.*

1. *Market Logic* (The Institute for Econometric Research, 3471 North Federal Highway, Fort Lauderdale, FL, 33306, $200/year) uses an econometric model to mathematically weight dozens of fundamental, technical, monetary and sentiment indicators to determine the major trend of the stock market. The model is very long term in nature (see figure 6.13) as it ignores both short and intermediate term market movements. The newsletter is published twice a month and has an excellent "Indicator Review" section that concisely provides the status of numerous important indicators. The subscription includes a telephone hotline.

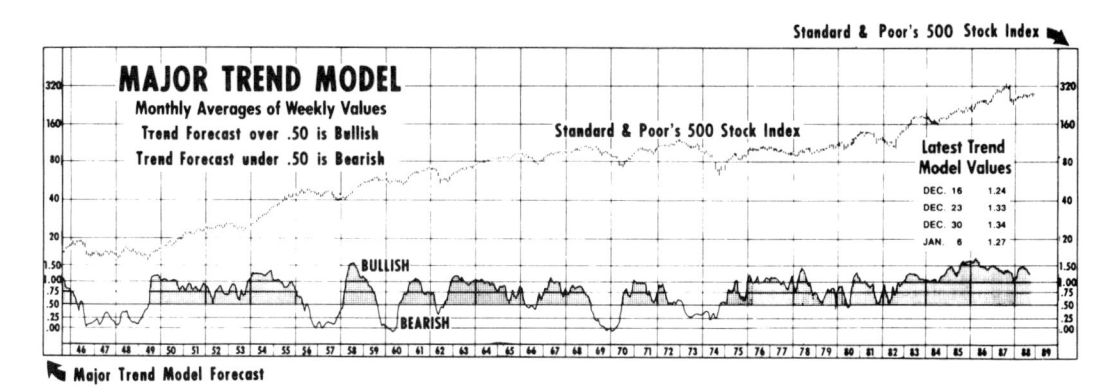

Figure 6.13. Market Logic Major Trend Model. From *Market Logic,* 3471 N. Federal Highway, Fort Lauderdale, FL 33306. Reprinted with permission.

2. *Paul Merriman's Fund Exchange* (PM & A, 1200 Westlake Avenue N., Suite 507, Seattle, WA 98109–3530) This monthly newsletter with hotline provides three timing models. The stock models are used to generate buy and sell signals for stock-to-money market transfers. Each of the three multi-factor models operate independently of one another. Following the advice of the newsletter allows the investor to ease in and ease out of stocks as market conditions change. Figure 6.14 shows how the Merriman system has worked over the past ten years, when applied to mutual funds. Although the record is shown on mutual funds, the Merriman timing system is applicable to the CREF stock, CREF Indexed Portfolio and CREF Bond funds. The gold timing portfolio shown is not of use for making TIAA-CREF TRANSFERS since a similar product to the United Services Gold Shares is not available.

3. *No-Load Portfolios* (527 Hotel Plaza, Boulder City, NV 89005, $69 per year). Edited by the authors of this book, the newsletter tracks numerous stock market timing models, as well as bond and gold switch models. All timing models are for long-term investing, and all but the gold fund are appropriate for making retirement fund transfers. Figure 6.15 provides a description of the models used. A weekly hotline is included with the newsletter.

4. *Systems and Forecasts* (The Signalert Corporation, 150 Great Neck Road, Great Neck, N.Y. 10021, $175 per year) is a fifteen year old newsletter that bases its market timing signals on a number of indicators that have been created with the help of computer software. Figure 6.16 shows the peformance of their latest timing model, which they call Time-Trend III. The model is an outgrowth of their previous timing Models I and II. This service also provides other timing models, such as their breadth-momentum oscillator and monetary filter (see figure 6.17). A telephone hotline keeps subscribers posted between issues of the newsletter.

5. *Timer Digest* (Timer Digest newsletter, P.O. Box 7700, Greenwich, CT 06836-7700) is a publication that provides the current status of stock market timing signals generated from many difference timing systems. They also provide the status of their own market timing system called CASPER (Computer Assisted Security and Portfolio Evaluation Reports). This timing system has been fully operational since 1980. Figure 6.18 graphically shows buy and sell signals for a two year period for the CASPER system.

	Fidelity Magellan					**Value Line Special Situations**			
Year	Buy/Hold		Market Timing		Year	Buy/Hold		Market Timing	
1970	−15.7%	$ 8,430	24.5%	$ 12,450	1970	−34.4%	$ 6,560	10.5%	$ 11.050
1971	35.1	11,389	31.7	16,397	1971	17.6	7,715	35.9	15,017
1972	30.1	14,817	28.9	21,135	1972	−11.0	6,866	−4.5	14,341
1973	−42.1	8,579	−7.5	19,550	1973	−45.5	3,742	−1.6	14,112
1974	−28.3	6,151	7.9	21,094	1974	−29.5	2,638	7.9	15,227
1975	44.4	8,882	23.5	26,051	1975	47.0	3,878	34.0	20,404
1976	35.5	12,035	32.4	34,492	1976	52.7	5,922	57.8	32,197
1977	16.3	13,997	4.4	36,010	1977	12.3	6,650	3.5	33,324
1978	31.7	18,434	26.4	45,517	1978	21.2	8,060	17.0	38,990
1979	51.7	27,964	26.9	57,761	1979	43.6	11,575	26.0	49,127
1980	69.9	47,511	74.3	100,677	1980	54.4	17,871	78.4	86,642
1981	16.4	55,303	20.4	121,215	1981	−2.2	17,478	8.5	95.092
1982	48.1	81,904	43.1	173,459	1982	23.1	21,515	30.7	124,285
1983	38.6	113,519	35.8	235,557	1983	19.4	25,689	21.4	150,882
1984	2.0	115,789	10.3	259,819	1984	−25.5	19,138	−5.7	142,282
1985	43.1	165,694	40.5	365,046	1985	−21.1	23,176	19.3	169.742
1986	23.7	204,963	16.5	425,279	1986	5.1	24,358	−7.5	157,011
1987	1.0	207,013	23.8	526,495	1987	−9.1	22,141	19.4	187,471
1988	22.7	254,005	8.7	572,300	1988	3.3	22,872	− 7.6	173,223

	Dreyfus Tax-Exempt Bond Fund					**United Services Gold Shares**			
Year	Buy/Hold		Market Timing		Year	Buy/Hold		Market Timing	
1978	−3.0%	$ 9,700	3.5%	$ 10,350	1975	−38.9%	$ 6,110	−5.3%	$ 9,470
1979	−1.4	9,564	6.3	11,002	1976	−41.1	3599	5.0	9,944
1980	−14.3	8,197	22.9	13,522	1977	39.9	5,035	11.8	11,117
1981	−10.0	7,377	6.6	14,414	1978	9.0	5,488	−8.4	10,183
1982	39.6	10,298	24.4	17,931	1979	187.2	15,762	142.6	24,704
1983	4.6	10,772	13.6	20,370	1980	78.9	28,198	78.4	44,072
1984	8.7	11,709	10.3	22,468	1981	−28.0	20,303	1.1	44,557
1985	19.4	13,981	18.5	26,625	1982	72.4	35,002	107.6	92,500
1986	17.3	16,400	10.7	29,470	1983	1.0	35,352	6.3	98,328
1987	−1.7	16,022	14.0	33,965	1984	−29.6	24,888	1.0	99,311
1988	11.5	17,865	8.8	36,954	1985	−26.8	18,218	−21.7	77,760
					1986	37.9	25,123	28.7	100,077
					1987	31.4	33,011	22.2	122,294
					1988	−35.7	21,226	−8.9	111,410

IMPORTANT NOTES
1) Paul A. Merriman & Associates (PM&A) started managing funds with the Merriman Equity Bond and Gold Switch Models on July 31, 1983; 2) The Models are hypothetically applied to the funds prior to July 31, 1983; 3) Average 90-day U.S. Treasury Bill rates are assumed while in money market funds; 4) Results do not include taxes or management fees; 5) The study assumes dividends and capital gains are reinvested; 6) Past results are no guarantee of future profitability. Reproduced with permission, Paul A. Merriman & Associates, 1200 Westlake Avenue North, Suite 507, Seattle, WA 98109-3530. (206)285-8877.

Figure 6.14. Merriman Timing Model Results vs. Buy and Hold. Reproduced with permission, Paul A. Merriman & Associates, 1200 Westlake Avenue North, Suite 507, Seattle, WA 98109–3530. (206)–285–8877.

1. *Moving average with confirmation* When the Investor's Daily Fund Index crosses its 200 day moving average, and this is confirmed by *either* a 200 day moving average crossing of the Dow Jones Industrials or Transportation index, a transfer signal is given.

2. *Interest Rates* When long term interest rates reverse trend either by crossing their 40 week exponential moving average or reverse in value by four percent (which ever happens first), a transfer signal is given.

3. *Institutional Money Flow* If large block volume is tending to make stocks rise, a favorable period of stock sponsorship is defined. If large block volume is tending to make stocks fall, a period is defined where a lack of institutional sponsorship exists. Transfers to stock is only permitted during the favorable stock sponsorship periods.

4. *Inflation adjusted Money Supply* Favorable and unfavorable periods for investment are defied by tracking the inflation adjusted rate of change of money supply (M2). When this liquidity measure is in an uptrend stocks are purchased, but *only* if the positive stock volume trend is favorable *or* a 4 percent reversal in the NYSE index occurs.

5. *Strategic Stock Model* This model is composed of four factors; 1) Federal Reserve Action, 2) money supply trend, 3) price-volume trend of the overall market, 4) direction of the U.S. dollar. Each factor is given a weighted score and the composite is used for generating timing signals.

6. *Advance-decline Indicator* A 40 week moving average of advancing minus declining issues is used to define favorable and unfavorable stock trends (This is a longer term version of the advance-decline indicator described earlier in this chapter).

7. *Yield Curve* The status of the yield curve *and* Federal Reserve tightening or loosening actions are used to generate stock timing signals. Both indicators must be in a favorable position for stocks to be purchased.

8. *Pressure Indicator* The difference between the Discount Rate and the T-Bill interest rate are used to forecast periods of coming tightening or loosening of credit. Forecasts of loose credit are seen as favorable to stocks, forecasts of tight credit are seen as unfavorable to stocks. Stocks are purchased during the favorable periods.

Figure 6.15. No-Load Portfolios Timing Models

PERFORMANCE RESULTS: TRADING THE NYSE INDEX ON TIME TREND III LONG SIDE ONLY, 1970–1988

Year	Profitable Trades	Unprofit-able Trades	Points Gained	Points Lost	Net Grain/Loss	Percentage Gain/Loss	Buy and Hold Point Change	Buy and Hold Percent Change
1970	5	1	+12.00	−1.89	+10.11	+24.5%	−1.87	−3.6%
1971	5	6	+14.63	−3.82	+10.81	+21.1%	+6.20	+12.3%
1972	8	4	+14.33	−3.28	+11.05	+19.9%	+8.05	+14.3%
1973	11	5	+15.12	−3.52	+11.60	+22.5%	−12.66	−19.6%
1974	6	7	+9.55	−9.12	+.43	+1.3%	−15.69	−30.3%
1975	7	2	+16.47	−2.31	+14.16	+39.8%	+11.51	+31.9%
1976	9	2	+15.29	−1.09	+14.20	+30.6%	+10.24	+21.5%
1977	8	8	+6.07	−8.17	−2.10	−3.7%	−5.38	−9.3%
1978	7	4	+12.32	−2.08	+10.24	+20.8%	+1.12	+2.1%
1979	10	1	+17.00	−.33	+16.67	+33.4%	+8.33	+15.5%
1980	5	1	+22.64	−1.44	+21.20	+35.5%	+15.91	+25.7%
1981	5	7	+12.23	−6.17	+6.06	+9.0%	−6.75	−8.7%
1982	5	9	+25.26	−7.95	+17.31	+28.0%	+9.92	+14.0%
1983	4	2–1 ev	+14.35	−.78	+13.57	+16.8%	+14.15	+17.5%
1984	7	9	+15.69	−8.59	+7.10	+8.0%	+1.20	+1.3%
1985	2	1	+28.57	−.75	+27.82	+29.3%	+25.20	+26.2%
1986	5	4	+24.32	−5.52	+18.80	+15.6%	+17.00	+14.0%
1987	5	4	+52.17	−11.67	+40.50	+29.5%	−.35	−0.3%
1988	6	2	$27.67	−2.77	+24.90	+18.4%	+18.58	+13.4%
	121(60.2%)	79(39.3%)	+355.68	−81.25	+274.43	+400.3%	+104.71	+137.9%

TIME-TREND III has produced a total gain of 274.43 points, an annual compounded rate of return of 20.8% per year, trading the NYSE Index, long side only. These results do not include dividend income while in the market, or interest income while in cash. Nor are potential short sale profits included.

Profit/loss ratios came to 4.38. 4.38 points were gained for every point lost.

Buy and hold strategies would have produced a net gain of +104.71 points, 6.1% compounded rate of return. Results are hypothetical through May 1988. Future results cannot be guaranteed but during the period tested TIME-TREND III outperformed buy and hold during 18 of 19 years, (falling behind only during 1983 (+16.8% versus +17.5%).

Figure 6.16a. Time-Trend III Performance Record. From *Systems and Forecasts*, the Signalert Corporation, 150 Great Neck Road, Great Neck, NY 11021. ($175.00 per year). Reprinted with permission.

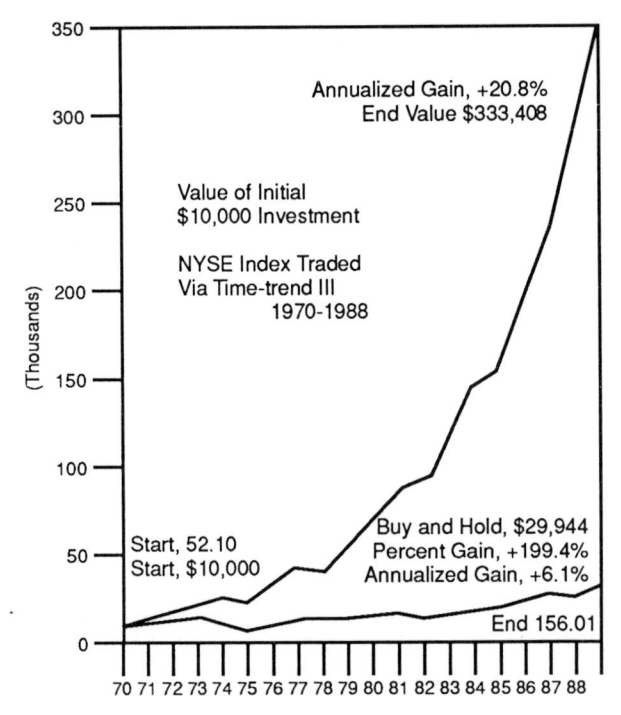

Figure 6.16b Time Trend Graph

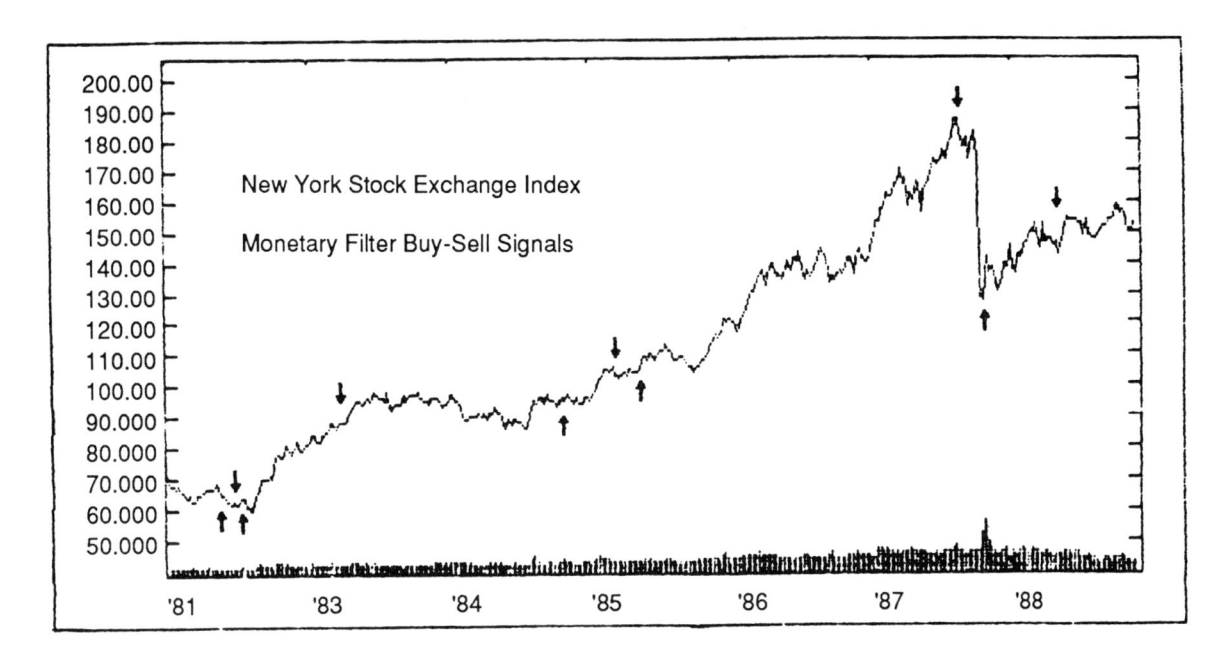

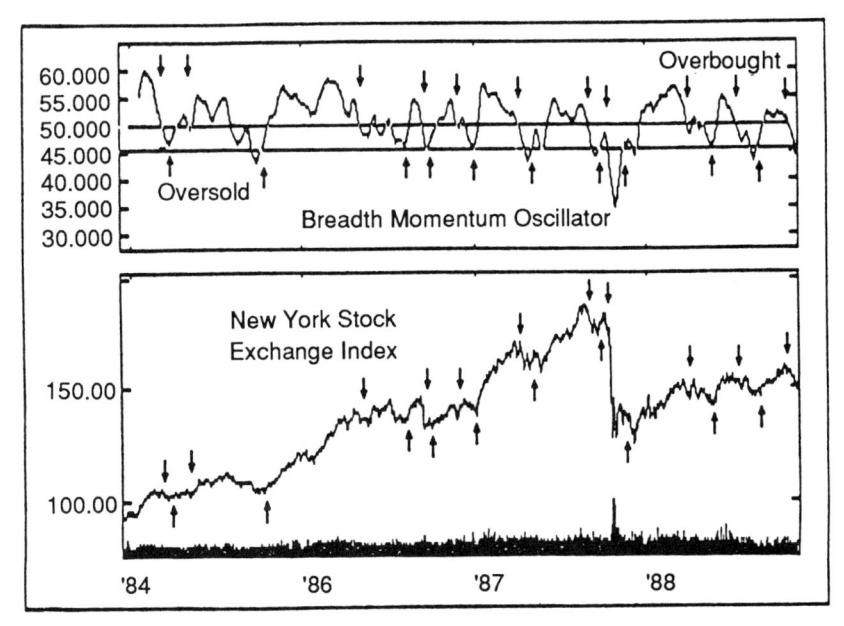

Figure 6.17. Systems and Forecasts Momentum Oscillator and Monetary Filter Models. From *Systems and Forecasts,* The Signalert Corporation, 150 Great Neck Road, Great Neck, NY 11021. ($175.00 per year). Reprinted with permission.

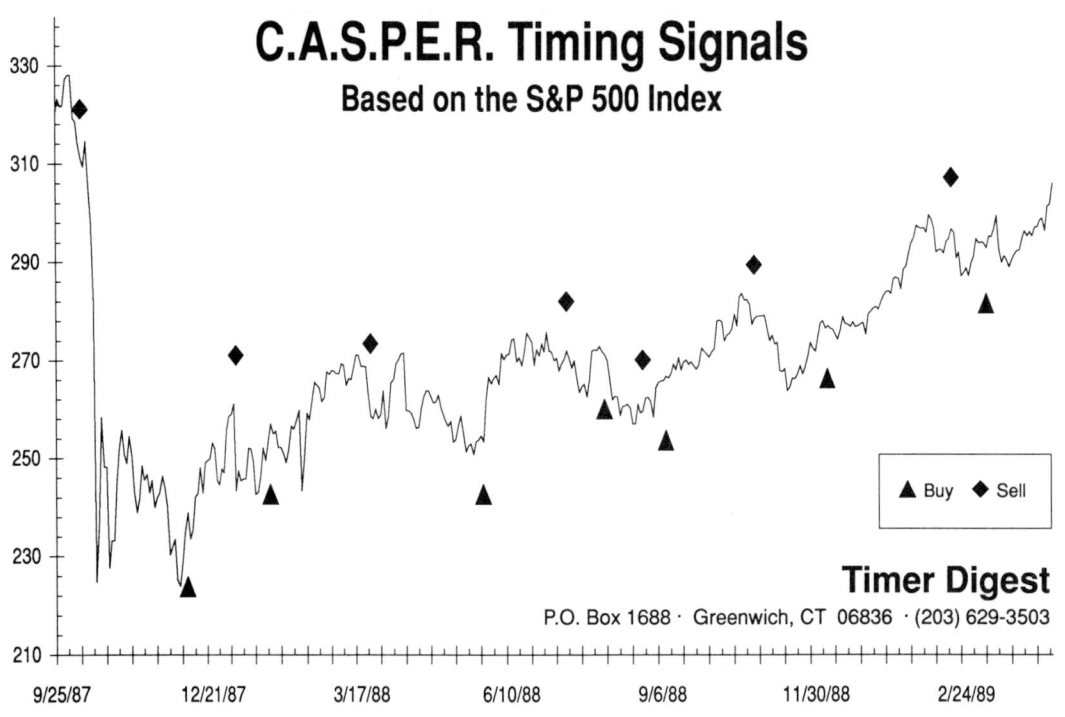

Figure 6.18. Casper Timing Signals. Reproduced with permission of Timer Digest, P.O. Box 1688, Greenwich, CT 06836–1688. Subscription phone: 800–356–2527.

Bibliography

Colby, Robert and Meyers, Thomas, *The Encyclopedia of Technical Market Indicators,* Dow Jones-Irwin, 1988.

Corney, William, *Dynamic Stock Market Analysis,* Dow Jones-Irwin, 1986.

Hirsch, Yale, *Don't Sell Stock on Monday,* Facts on File Publications, 1986.

Stoken, Richard A. *Strategic Investment Timing,* Macmillan, 1984.

Veilleux, Eugene, *How to Switch Your Money Market Fund for Maximum Profit,* E. D. Veilleux, 1983.

Zweig, Martin, *Martin Zweig's Winning with New IRA's,* Warner Books, 1987.

Chapter 7

The New TIAA-CREF Offerings

TIAA-CREF's new investment vehicle offerings include: 1) a bond fund, 2) a balanced fund, 3) an actively managed equities (stock) fund, 4) a passive equities (index) fund, and 5) an international equities fund.

With such a dazzling array of investment options it will be difficult for the average TIAA-CREF participant to know what to do. Fortunately, there is a way to make sense out of this investment maze. Knowledge of the business cycle can be used to provide a framework for assessing the risk and reward prospects for the various new investment offerings. As all of one's money should not be placed in any one investment vehicle, the business cycle helps to indicate the appreciation potential of various investment allocations over time.

The Business Cycle

Instead of growing smoothly over time, our economy goes through repeated periods of expansion and contraction. Each expansion—contraction cycle typically lasts about four to six years, so two full cycles can be expected every ten years or so. Why do these cycles exist? Why can't our economy keep expanding without going through a contraction (recession) phase?

As the economy grows, excess labor and productive capacity are put to use. This results in improved productivity and higher profits for business. Increased employment means more money in pockets and purses available for spending, which in turn means a greater demand for products and services. Manufacturing businesses respond by increasing production. The service industry expands to meet the increased demand by hiring more service personnel. Unfortunately the good times do not last forever, as a series of developments plant the seeds for an eventual downturn.

As the expansion continues, new participants are lured into the business scene. More and more money is available for investing, and making money appears almost easy. Eventually, as the pace of economic activity quickens, it becomes difficult for business to expand further without being subjected to increased costs. Competent additional employees may be difficult to obtain without offering higher wages, and overtime wages may have to be paid to existing employees. Moreover, additional new facilities may have to be built to meet demand. The result is an "overheating" in the economy with an increase in inflation arising from the higher business costs.

When inflation increases, the Federal Government gets worried. Not only is inflation a bad thing in itself, but it forces the Government into actions they'd rather not take. Many payment programs (Social Security, for example), are indexed to the inflation rate. As inflation rises, the government must meet its obligations and increase payments, putting pressure on the budget deficit. The value of the U.S. dollar is also affected adversely by an increase in the inflation rate, and the government does not want a depreciating dollar. To avoid these problems, the Federal Reserve Board responds to the rising inflation by raising short-term interest rates.

As we mentioned in chapter 6, a rise in short-term interest rates has the effect of eventually slowing down the economic expansion. This is because higher interest rates make it more costly and difficult to borrow money, and this acts as a brake to the economy. From the consumer's point of view, higher rates mean credit card balances cost more each month to carry. For home owners with variable rate mortgages, it means higher payments and less money available to invest or make purchases. For businesses, higher rates mean great difficulty in qualifying for bank loans and higher monthly costs if the loans can be obtained. In short, the expansionary part of the business cycle is choked off by the higher interest borrowing costs.

In theory it might be possible for the Federal Reserve to slow the economy down, reduce inflationary pressures, then let it expand again without the onset of a recession. This is called an economic "soft landing". In practice, the economy is difficult to control this precisely. The result of higher interest rates is usually a mild to severe recession. Once a recession is evident, the Federal Reserve drops interest rates in an attempt to stimulate the economy and pull it out of its poor condition. This sets the stage for the next economic expansion and the start of the next cycle. This repeating cycle holds the key to knowing what investments are best to make at different times.

Investments and Business Cycle Phases

As a TIAA-CREF Retirement plan participant, you should keep this economic cycle in mind when making decisions on how to allocate your money. By investing with the cycle instead of against it, you can increase your odds of success.

During different phases of the business cycle, different investments have preferred periods of time when they tend to do well. Figure 7.1 sums-up the relationship between types of investments and the previously discussed business cycle.

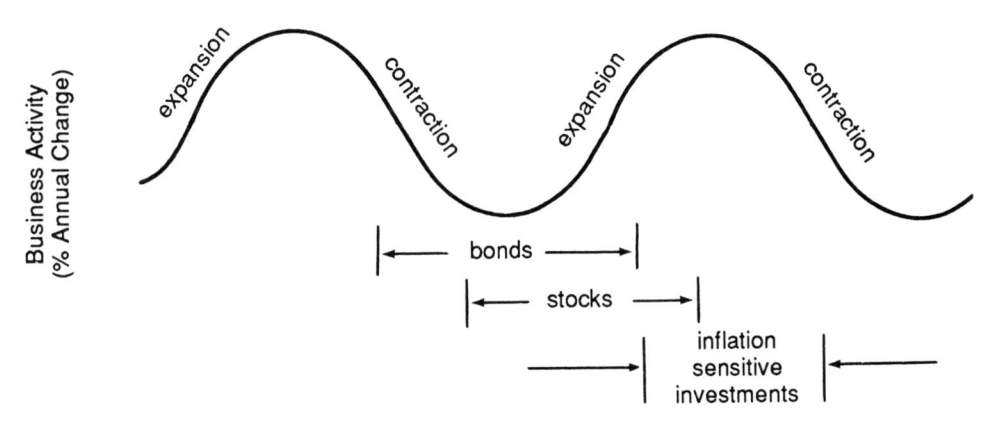

Figure 7.1. Investments and the Business Cycle

The figure shows two complete business cycles; expansion—contraction, and again, expansion—contraction. Looking from the left side of the diagram to the right, as the economy loses steam and begins contracting, bonds tend to perform well. This is because interest rates fall as the Federal Reserve Board attempts to stimulate the economy. Falling rates mean bond price appreciation in addition to the interest generated by the bonds themselves. After the slowdown has been underway for a period of months, investors begin to look past the bad times to better days ahead, and the stock market begins to advance. This typically occurs about six months before the bottoming-out period. Stocks tend to do well throughout the expansion period, as corporate earnings are strong. The favorable period for bonds ends when interest rates begin rising, after the expansion period has matured and inflation becomes a perceived problem. Contemporary with the unfavorable period for bonds is the start of a favorable period for inflation hedges and money market funds. Inflation hedges do well because the inflation rate during this phase of the business cycle is increasing. Money market funds do well because of the high short-term interest rates which the Federal Reserve Bond engineers in an attempt to reduce the inflation rate.

The scenario just described tends to repeat itself over and over as the business cycle continues, so it can be used as a basic framework for making long-term investment decisions. Each individual cycle, however, tends to be unique in one way or another. How do the cycles differ? The time duration of expansions tends to vary considerably from cycle to cycle, with the shortest post-war expansionary period being 12 months (1980–1981) and the longest being 106 months (1961–1969).The level of inflation also has varied widely. In the more recent expansions, a higher level of inflation has generally been tolerated than in the past. For example, in the 1958–1960 expansion, an interest rate of 1.7 percent ended the expansion, while in the 1980–1981 expansion an inflation rate of 9.2 percent occurred.

A major recent factor causing business cycles to differ is the growing influence of foreign investors on our securities markets. As a country, we are less insulated from world events than ever before in history, and this has an impact on our economy and investments. Figure 7.2 shows how the movement of the U.S. dollar compares with the price movement of the U.S. stock market in the recent past. As the graph shows, movement of the U.S. dollar and the stock market are highly correlated.

As the dollar strengthens, foreigners are attracted to U.S. investments because they can get a "bonus" return from the appreciating currency.

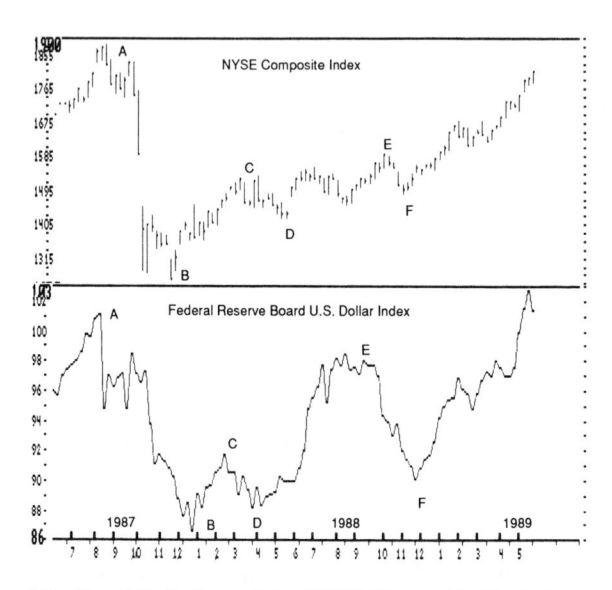

Figure 7.2. The U.S. Dollar and the NYSE Composite Stock Average.

This foreign demand helps move the market up. As the dollar weakens, foreign investment in U.S. markets becomes less attractive because of the loss from the unfavorable exchange rate trend. This reduction of foreign buying power helps to stall the stock market's advance.

What are the factors that move the dollar up or down? There are four that are important to keep in mind: 1) interest rate differences, 2) trade deficits, 3) inflation differences, and 4) speculation. If interest rates are higher in one country than in another, and all other important factors are the same, the currency with the higher interest rate will become more attractive and will be bid up by investors seeking a higher return than they can get in their own country. A large trade deficit means foreigners have excess currency from trade that they will want to do something with. Persistent selling to convert it to the local (or other) currency will drive the currency of the trade deficit country down. A country with a comparatively higher inflation rate will tend to have a depreciation of its currency to the extent that buying power is kept about the same in terms of other currencies. Finally, speculation by money traders based on expectations concerning future changes in any of the previously mentioned factors (and a host of others) can cause up and down movements in a currency's value.

What makes the dollar's movements so interesting in recent years is the previously mentioned link to stock prices. The correlation is strong because of the unprecedented prosperity enjoyed by foreign investors who rush in to buy when the dollar strengthens. This "hot" foreign money has the potential to change the way the market reacts to the domestic business cycle. For example, rising interest rates usually mean the end of an expansionary phase and trouble for stocks. For the U.S. dollar, however, rising rates means a stronger dollar, thereby potentially attracting foreign investment capital. This means it is possible for the stock market to rise substantially during the inflationary part of the business cycle *if* the rising interest rates strengthen the dollar and *if* a large demand for U.S. stocks from foreign sources exist.

The point is that you can never be absolutely sure in advance how the market will perform, despite the overall similarities of individual business cycles. A probabilistic attitude toward investment decision making is therefore a necessity. With this in mind, the "trick" for allocating CREF investment dollars is to develop a multifactor system that tracks the major business cycle influences. We can hope for perfection but know the best we can ever do is to attempt to put the odds for success in our favor. The wrong approach is to guess when to buy or sell, and transfer all of our money between accounts on the basis of guesswork. Diversifying by splitting investment money into parts and using differing strategies for the various parts will avoid potential disaster and pay off in the long term.

Let's now look at each of the new TIAA-CREF accounts in turn to see how they can be managed, within the business cycle framework.

The CREF Bond Account

Bonds are debt instruments issued by public and private organizations for the purpose of raising money. They pay the lender an interest rate that in part reflects the risk inherent in the issue. A new start-up electronics company, for example, would have to pay a higher interest rate to borrow money than the U.S. government would, because potential purchasers want to be compensated for the increased risk of default. Bond funds also carry two kinds of risk other than the risk of default; market risk and call (prepayment) risk. Market risk is the potential for fluctuation in the bonds' principal value based on changing levels of market interest rates. As we mentioned previously, as interest rates in the economy rise, the principal value of bonds currently in existence fall, in order to adjust their total rate of return to the reality of the higher interest rate market. If this did not happen, there would be no way to sell old bonds that provide a lower interest rate than the prevailing (market) rate. Call (prepayment) risk is the chance that income producing securities will be redeemed by the insurer, so they can lower their borrowing cost.

The CREF bond account will reduce the default and prepayment risks by purchasing bonds from many sources and with differing dates of maturity and other diversifying characteristics. The negative effect on total return from these sources of risk can therefore be expected to be minimal. Reducing market risk is another story, however, as little can be done if interest rates suddenly rise. Figure 7.3 provides an indication of expected changes in the bond fund's value for selected changes in market interest rates.

The figure indicates that during the times of the business cycle when interest rates are rising, bonds are poor investments since their principal value will drop. However, just the opposite is true during times when interest rates are falling; not only do the bonds continue to earn interest but their principle value also increases. The exact amount of change in principle value depends on the fund's average maturity, which is established by CREF management. Lets look at some methods that can be used to identify the favorable periods and avoid the unfavorable ones.

If Interest Rates Change by 2 Percentage Points

	8% Bond Coupon		10 % Bond Coupon	
years to maturity	rates rise	rates fal	rates rise	rates fall
1	−1.9%	+1.9%	−1.8%	+1.9%
5	−7.7%	+8.5%	−7.4%	+8.1%
10	−12.5%	+14.9%	−11.5%	+13.6%
15	−15.4%	+19.6%	−13.8%	+17.3%

If Interest Rates Change by 4 Percentage Points

	8% Bond Coupon		10 % Bond Coupon	
years to maturity	rates rise	rates fall	rates rise	rates fall
1	−3.7%	+3.9%	−3.6%	+3.8%
5	−14.7%	+18.0%	−14.1%	+17.1%
10	−22.9%	+32.7%	−21.2%	+29.8%
15	−27.5%	+44.8%	−26.7%	+46.2%

Figure 7.3. Changes in Bond Fund Value for Changes in Market Interest Rates

Defining Interest Rate Trends to Establish Buy and Sell Points

A simple way to determine when interest rates are rising (bad for bonds) or falling (good for bonds) is to use a moving average system. Figure 7.4 shows an example of how this can be done.

Weekly "best bonds" data from *Barron's* magazine are used, with a 40 week moving average chosen to define long term trends while ignoring the short term movements. With this system, when interest rates decline (move down through the moving average), the bond fund is purchased. Conversely, when rates move up through the moving average the bond fund is sold. The CREF money market account is used as the interest generating depositary for money when the bond fund is sold. As the figure shows, this method can keep you on the right side of the interest rate trend. It takes only a few seconds each week to keep up this system if financial computer software is available (see chapter 6 for software options). Of course the mathematics can be done manually. The manual method shown in the previous chapter for calculating the moving average of advance-decline indicator can be used for this purpose.

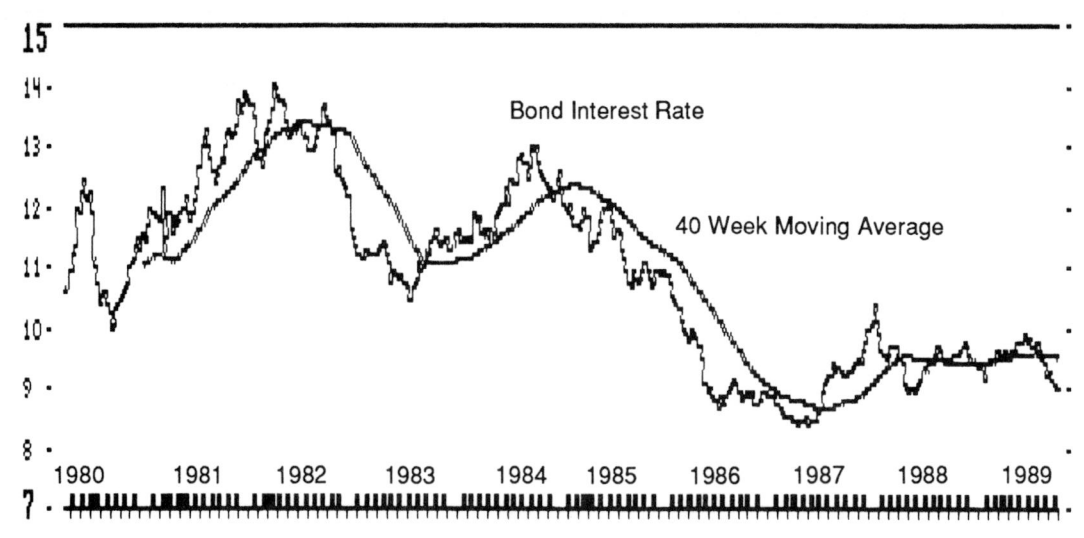

Figure 7.4. Moving Average Trend Defining System

Another way to define interest rate trends is to keep a close watch on the prime rate. The prime rate is the interest rate charged by banks to their best corporate borrowers. It tends to go up when the general level of interest rates in the economy goes up, and it tends to go down when the general level of interest rates are declining. The information about prime rate increases and decreases are widely disseminated when they occur. All major newspapers and national television news broadcasts indicate when the prime rate changes. The bond fund can be purchased when the prime rate reverses from going up to going down, and the fund can be sold when the prime rate reverses from going down to going up. Figure 7.5 shows the recent pattern of prime rate activity.

Other Ways to Time the Bond Fund

Besides simply tracking interest rates for generating buy and sell signals, there are other ways to determine favorable and unfavorable periods of bonds. One way is to construct a bond model. Like the models discussed in the previous chapter, the bond model attempts to tie together major factors that appear to be associated with the increase or decrease in bond prices. As an example, the Bond model used in the *No Load Portfolios* investment newsletter considers three factors; 1) the movement of bond prices themselves, 2) the inflation rate, and 3) the interest rate trend. Three model points are given when bond prices are moving up, two model points are given when inflation is moving down and two model points are given

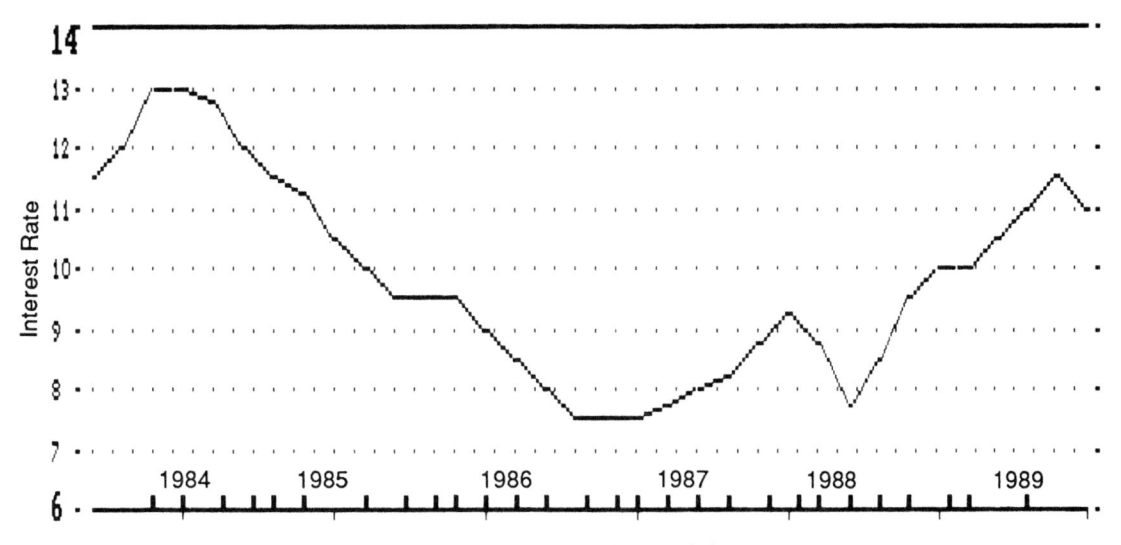

Figure 7.5. Recent Prime Rate Activity

when interest rates are moving down. When each of these factors are moving in the opposite (unfavorable) directions, no points are given. When the sum of model points reaches five or more, a buy signal is given. When points sum to less than five, bonds are sold. This model uses a 40 week exponential average with the Dow Jones 20 bond average to determine the direction of bonds (most technical software easily calculates this type of moving average). The inflation rate direction is found using the wholesale inflation rate (producer price index) and a 10 month moving average to define the trend. The direction of interest rates is determined using prime rate increases and decreases as discussed in the previous section.

Another bond model for consideration is described in Martin Zweig's book, *Winning With New IRA's*. This model uses two indicators to determine the movement of the Dow Jones 20 Bond Index, an indicator to determine Federal Reserve policy, and a yield curve indicator that compares short and long term interest rates. Each of the four indicators in the model is worth +1 point in a favorable position and -1 point when in an unfavorable position. When the sum of points reaches +3 a buy signal is given. When it reaches -3 a sell signal is given. For further details on the construction of this model we refer you to Martin Zweigs' book.

TIAA-CREF participants that would like to buy timing signals for the CREF bond account may want to consider subscribing to Davis/Zweig's *Bond Fund Timer* (Davis/Zweig Futures, Inc. P.O. Box 5345, New York, N.Y. 10150), or Martin Pring's *The Interest Rate Review* (Interest Rate Review, International Institute for Economic Research, PO Box 329,

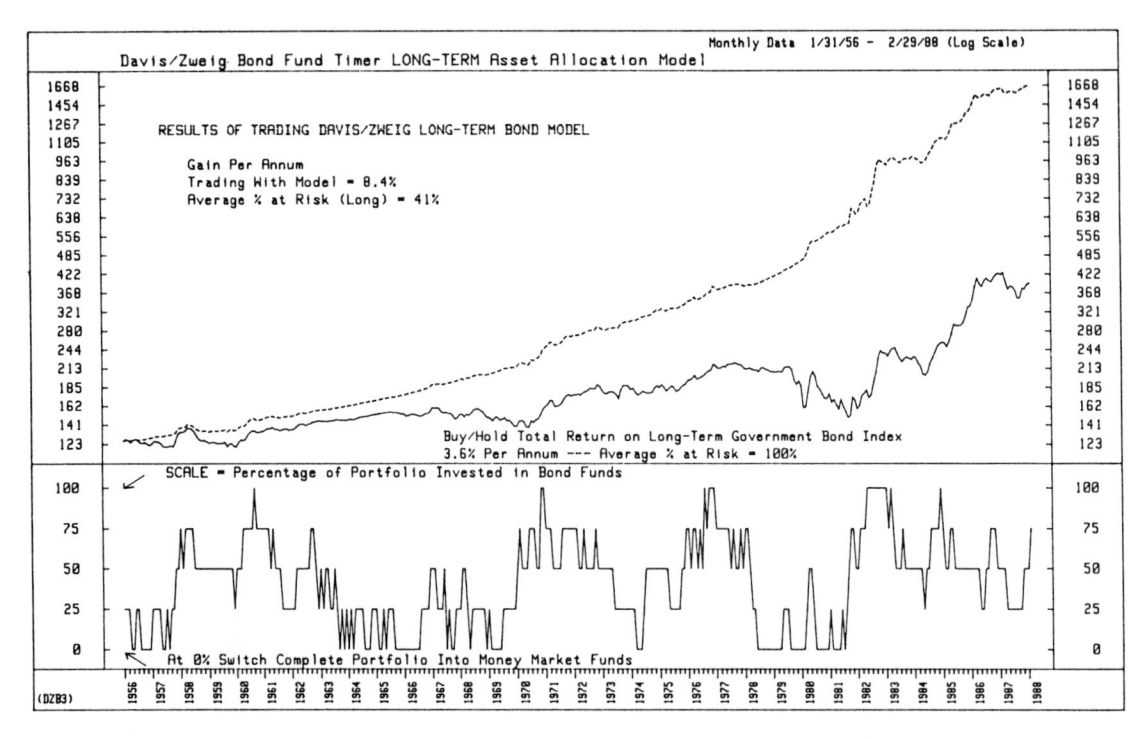

Figure 7.6. Davis/Zweig Bond Fund Timer. From *Davis/Zweig Bond Fund Timer,* Davis/Zweig Futures, Inc. P.O. Box 360, New York, N.Y. 11710. Reprinted with permission.

Blackville Road, Washington Depot, CT 06794, $195 per year). Figures 7.6 and 7.7 shows results of the Zweig and Pring Models. It is interesting to note that the Davis/Zweig model uses an incremental approach to transfer money between bond and money market investments (0%, 25%, 50%, 75% and 100% increments). As you know, this is the fundamental approach to making transfers that we recommend in this book.

The CREF Balanced Account

The basic idea behind a balanced account is to lower the overall volatility of a portfolio of securities by investing in both stocks and bonds. This mix lowers the volatility of the portfolio because stocks and bonds do not go up and down in value at the same time. As we indicated before, when a business slow-down occurs, interest rates drop, propelling bonds upward. At the same time, the uncertainty over the level of earnings during a business slowdown often causes a decline in equities. Conversely, during the expansionary period when stocks do well, interest rates usually rise, lowering the value of bonds. It is the way stocks and bonds move during the business cycle that makes a balanced portfolio "work". By holding a

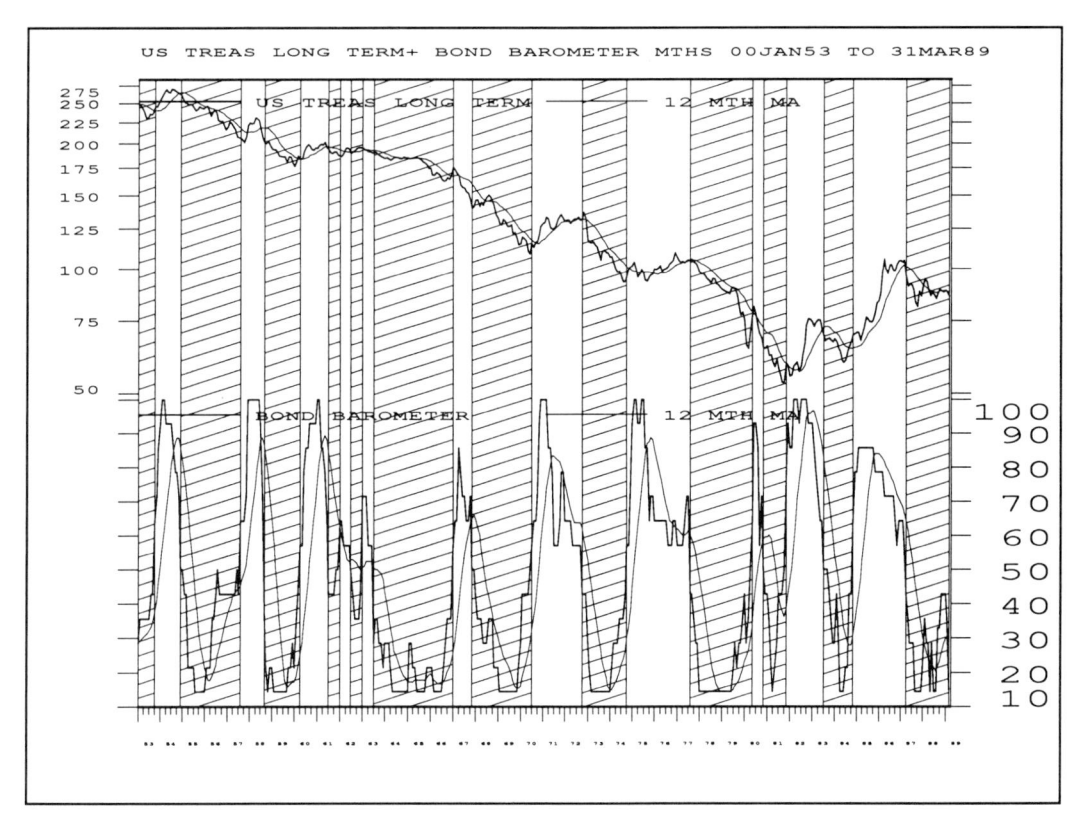

Figure 7.7. Martin Pring's Bond Timer Model. From *The Interest Rate Review,* P.O. Box 329, Blackville Rd., Washington Depot, CT 06794 ($195 per year). Reprinted with permission.

balanced fund, the total volatility is reduced, while maintaining a reasonable long-term rate of return.

Figure 7.8 shows the well known stock-bond "C-curve" which indicates the historical relationship between volatility and return for various percentages of stocks and bonds in a portfolio. The bottom point on the curve represents the risk-return point for a portfolio consisting of 100 percent bonds, and the upper end of the curve represents the risk-return point for a portfolio consisting of 100 percent stocks. All other points along the curve represent combinations of stocks and bonds in differing proportions.

Surprisingly, research has shown that a portfolio holding about 35 percent bond and 65 percent stocks has approximately the same volatility as one holding 100 percent bonds. The pleasant difference is that the stock and bond portfolio has an average annual return about two and one-half percent greater than bonds alone. It should be noted that the highest annual return is from 100 percent stocks, but this also provides the greatest

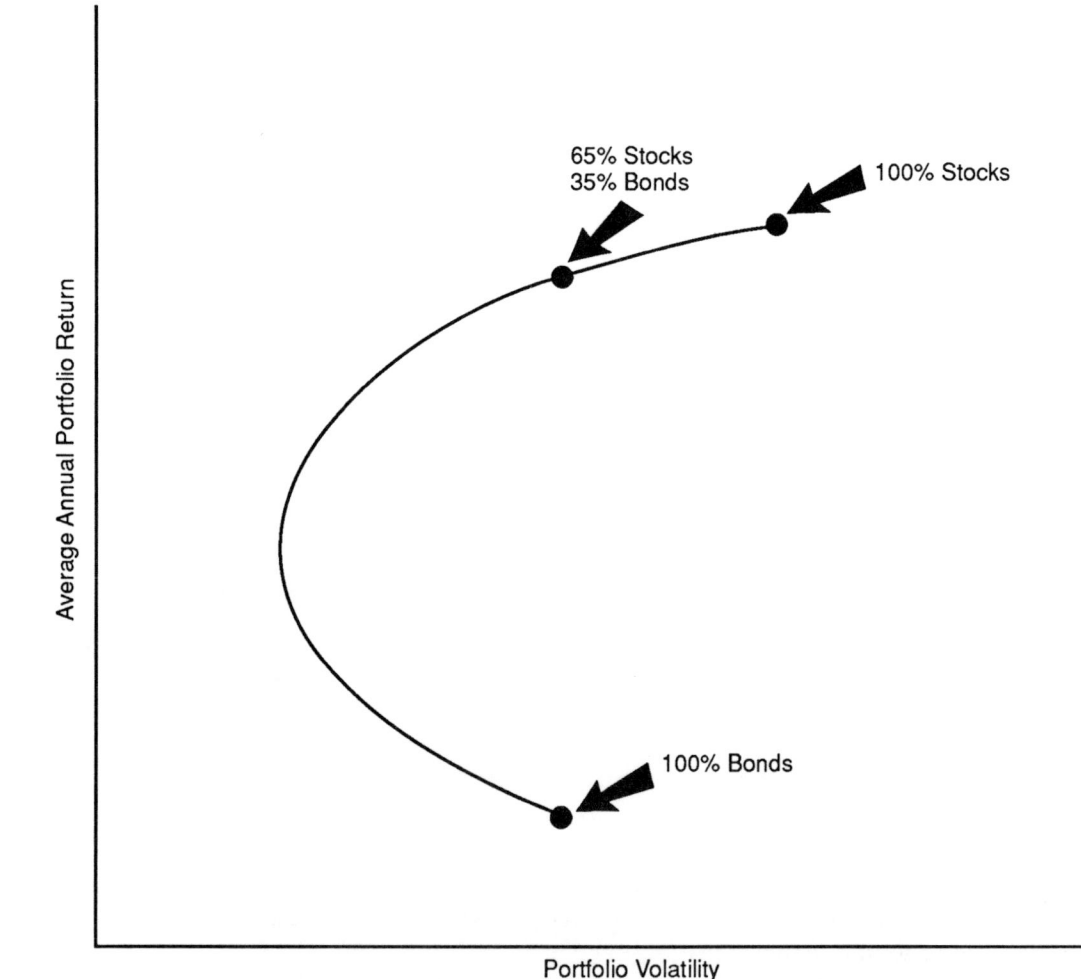

Figure 7.8. Stock-Bond Combinations, Rate of Return and Volatility

volatility. This historical relationship is the theoretical foundation upon which balanced funds are based.

As you can guess, it is possible to create your own "balanced fund" by holding the CREF stock account and CREF bond account in proportions approximating the low risk-high yield point shown in figure 7.8. What the CREF balanced account management will do for you is to actively manage the stock-bond ratio throughout the business cycle to produce the highest return at a reasonable risk level. This may require variation in the proportions of stocks and bonds held, as well as changes in the interest rate sensitivity of the mix of corporate stocks in the portfolio. In short, it is the actions of CREF Balanced account management that potentially provides greater value than a simple mixing of CREF stock and CREF bond portfolios.

TIAA-CREF participants with a low risk tolerance who in the past have been oriented almost exclusively to TIAA should consider placing some monthly allocation in the Balanced Portfolio. This will provide some of the long-term advantages of owning stocks, while reducing the volatility inherent from holding stocks alone. The balanced fund can be expected to work best if it is held over many business cycles instead of being bought and sold frequently. A long-term dollar averaging approach with this fund is therefore recommended (see chapter 5).

CREF International Account

In the 1960's both the Dow Jones Industrial Average and the Tokyo Dow reached 1000. Today, while the U.S. Dow is under 3000, the Tokyo Dow is over 30,000. Moreover, as the Tokyo Dow was making its spectacular move, the Yen tripled in value against the U.S. Dollar. Long-term investors in the Japanese market were so well rewarded because of the phenomenal rate of growth experienced by Japanese businesses. Other economic miracles can be expected to take place in the future as less-developed countries are transformed into modern economies and the newly emerging countries continue to expand. Besides the free world economies, we are now witnessing major changes in their economic aspects of communism in Eastern Europe, Russia, and China. As their economies take on more free-market aspects and begin expanding, we can expect them to import more and more western goods and provide fertile ground for multinational manufacturing facilities from around the world. Moreover, the integration of the European economic community in 1992 will offer a vast market for goods and services of all types, providing more opportunities for world growth. In short, investment opportunities around the world are greater now than ever before, and the trend will likely continue into the future.

The "downside" of international investing is that volatility may be greater than that experienced with U.S. stocks. The business cycle is more pronounced in many foreign countries and many do not have the kind of political stability that we are accustomed to here. Moreover, government regulations are different across countries, so a companies' long-term future may be more difficult to assess. Finally, differing accounting procedures and disclosure rules sometimes makes it impossible to really know the value of a foreign company and how it is doing. These factors make foreign stock selection difficult for the portfolio managers as well as individual investors.

The bottom line is that foreign investment offers potential growth rates in excess of what we may experience here at home in the U.S., but greater risk comes along with the higher expected return. CREF management will attempt to participate in the high growth potential at a "reasonable" risk level that comes from diversification by both company and country. All things said, a TIAA-CREF participant with a long term perspective and above average risk orientation may wish to make use of the international fund for a portion of retirement investments.

How much money should be placed in the international fund and how should it be timed for purchase? It is our feeling that for the investor willing to live with the greater risk, somewhere between 10 and 20 percent of total funds should be allocated to the international fund. The best timing technique is straight dollar cost averaging—have purchases made each month and either leave the total alone or use an allocation strategy like one discussed in chapter 4. The reason for not attempting to trade international fund accumulations is because of the difficulty in constructing a rational transfer system. A myriad of factors influence the overall performance of the fund, including dollar exchange rates, business cycles of the various countries in the fund, political concerns, the investment mix, and numerous other factors which when taken together make timing difficult.

For those who want to trade the fund anyway, we suggest timing transfers with the CREF money market account. The only feasible approach is to use a long-term moving average (for example, 40 weeks) on the fund's per unit price values, obtained on a weekly basis by calling TIAA-CREF for a quote. When the unit value exceeds the moving average value it should be purchased, when it falls below the moving average it should be sold and the proceeds transferred to the CREF money market account.

The CREF Passive Equities (Index) Account

The CREF Passive Equities fund is designed to match the up and down movements of the overall stock market by buying and holding a portfolio of stocks that mirror the action of the market as a whole. The long-term performance of the portfolio will therefore be about the same as that of stocks in a general sense. Since no stock picking ability or economic analysis is necessary to manage the account, the management fees should be less than that of the CREF Actively Managed stock account, to be discussed next. The fee difference will show up in the total return for the portfolio.

This new portfolio is a natural candidate for market based transfer systems discussed in chapter 6. It can also be used as part of a dollar cost averaging system like those described in chapter 5.

CREF Actively Managed Account

The goal of the CREF Actively Managed Account is appreciation of capital through rational stock selection procedures and through the timing of the purchase and sale of securities. The big question posed by this CREF offering is whether it offers additional value as compared with the older CREF Stock account.

As we learned from figure 6.7, the CREF Stock account is primarily indexed to the market, with less than 30 percent actively managed. This "limited management" approach has proved successful over the long run in doing slightly better than the overall market as measured by the S & P 500. Can we expect better performance than this from the actively managed account? Probably not.

While some great fund managers exist (Peter Lynch and John Templeton come to mind), the vast majority of fund managers are fortunate if they can simply match the performance of the overall market, let alone beat it over the long term. We think the most prudent course of action for a TIAA-CREF participant is to wait until the managers of this fund establish a track record. For adventurous participants, we suggest a small percentage (10 percent or less) allocated to this fund on a monthly basis until its performance record justifies a greater exposure.

Bibliography

CREF Prospectus and Statement of Additional Information, CREF, 1989.

"Progress Report on the Future Agenda", *The Participant,* August, 1988.

The American Association of Individual Investor's Guide to No-Load Mutual Funds, International Publishing Corporation, Chicago, 1989.

"Update on the New CREF options," *The Participant,* May, 1989.

Chapter 8

Using TIAA-CREF Services

TIAA-CREF offers a wealth of services to its participants, many of which are not generally known or understood. Our goal in this chapter is to show how you can use these services to your long-term benefit.

The chapter is organized into four major sections. We start by indicating how you can make sense of your TIAA-CREF statements. This is followed by a discussion of how to use the automated telephone service and when you should use it. The third section discusses retirement benefits and how to obtain them. Finally, we discuss the TIAA-CREF Supplemental Retirement Annuities.

Making Sense of Your Statements

TIAA-CREF participants receive a quarterly statement of transactions and accumulations, and an annual annuity benefits report.

The "bottom line" on the quarterly report is your total accumulation, found at the lower right-hand corner of the statement. The amount shown represents the total dollar value of your accumulation units as of the ending period date. If you were to retire immediately and choose to receive annuity income, this would be the amount available for purchasing TIAA-CREF annuities. This total also represents the amount your beneficiary would receive if you were to die. Because of its dual nature, the accumulation should be viewed as a dollar amount with both a potential annuity value and a current life insurance value. Because of the time needed to print and mail the statements, your total accumulation value probably does not reflect the latest month's contribution to your account. Moreover, the market value of securities have likely changed, so the total accumulation should be viewed only as indicating an approximate current value when the statement is received. (A precise accumulation value can be obtained at any time through use of the TIAA-CREF Automated Telephone Service. This will be discussed later in the chapter.)

The center box on your quarterly report titled, "Summary of Transactions this Quarter," contains information concerning contributions made during the period specified by the statement. The date the contributions were made, how your money was allocated among the various options, and the dollar amount of each option is also given. If you have any doubt concerning the accuracy of the listed contributions, you can check the amounts by matching the "Premiums" shown on the report with the amounts on your recent employer pay stubs.

The lower box on your quarterly report, titled "Changes in Annuity Accumulations this Quarter", should be read downward, from the top of the box to the bottom, for each TIAA-CREF account. It provides opening totals, what was added during the quarter, and resultant closing totals for TIAA and CREF accounts. The term "Unit Value" refers to the dollar price for each of the CREF units owned. This can be thought of in the same manner that a price per share is thought of in a mutual fund. In the same manner of thinking, the "Units" figure can be considered as similar to the number of shares of a mutual fund. Worthy of special notice is the "Interest" line in the TIAA accumulation box. This amount represents the interest on the financial instruments (mainly long term mortgages and other business loans) held by TIAA that have been credited to your account.

The other statement that you receive from TIAA-CREF is the "Anual Benefits Report", which provides a year-end account status and illustrates benefits that you would receive at retirement based on certain specified assumptions. Because of the long-term uncertainties concerning inflation rates, interest rates, stock price movements, and your future salary levels, the long-term projections are of limited value for most TIAA-CREF participants. As you get close to retirement, however, the illustrations will have greater meaning for you. If you want an income illustration based on a set of assumptions that are more realistic for your situation, TIAA-CREF will make a calculation for you at no cost (call 1-800-842-2776).

The hypothetical information in the report shows potential first-year benefits based on each of two options: the TIAA Level Benefit Method and the Graded Benefit method. The Level Benefit Method is the option you have of receiving all of your TIAA annuity dividends in full each year, while with the Graded Benefit Method, you only receive part of the dividends as a payout, with the rest being used to buy future income. This means that, all else being equal, your retirement check from TIAA under the graded benefit method can be expected to increase from year to year during your retirement. Advantages and disadvantages of these options will be discussed in detail in this chapter under the "Benefits Options" section.

Using the TIAA-CREF Automated Telephone Service

The Automated Telephone Service offers an easy way to accomplish any one of three tasks: 1) obtain a quote of the total value for any of your TIAA-CREF annuities, 2) make transfers of funds between accounts, and 3) change the allocation of future premiums. All three automated transactions can be accomplished with a touch tone phone 24 hours a day, 7 days a week. Transfer and allocation change instructions using the Automated Telephone Service are effective as of the close of the business day, if received before 4:00 P.M Eastern Time. Instructions after this time are effective at the close of the next business day. Transfer instructions and future allocation changes are confirmed in writing after processing.

To make use of the Automated Telephone Service you need a Personal Identification Number (PIN) and your appropriate contract number(s). Your contract numbers appear on both your quarterly and annual statements. TIAA-CREF has a PIN number assigned to all participants. If you have misplaced yours, call them to find out what it is. You should do this immediately, even if you do not plan to use the automated system soon.

When using the system, there are a few things to keep in mind from the start. First, it is important to get organized before attempting the call. Have your PIN and Contract numbers handy, along with accumulated annuity amounts, if this is important to your call. You should remember that after every entry is completed, the pound key (#) should be depressed to let the system know that your entry is complete. It is also important to recognize that part of the contract identifier is alphabetic. This is not a problem for most of the letters, as the buttons on touch-tone phones display letters as well as numbers. The letter "Q", however, is not displayed on the phone buttons, so, if you have this letter in your contract identifier, you have to pretend that the "Q" is there by pushing the key with the letters PRS on it. This is key number 7. TIAA-CREF also allows you to talk to one of their representatives if you would rather deal with a person than a machine. During off-business hours a voice-operated message recorder is available to handle calls from rotary phones.

Obtaining the Current Value of Your Annuities

To obtain the current value of your annuities, you have the option of listening to the automated dialogue or skipping it and getting your accumulated totals directly. Figure 8.1 details the later approach. The key to the fast method is the "*". It allows you to skip over the dialogue each time it is pressed.

STEPS

1. Phone: 1-800-842-2252

2. [#] [ ][ ][ ][ ][ ][ ] [*]
       (your PIN number)

3. [ ][ ][ ][ ][ ][ ][ ]
   (your contract number)

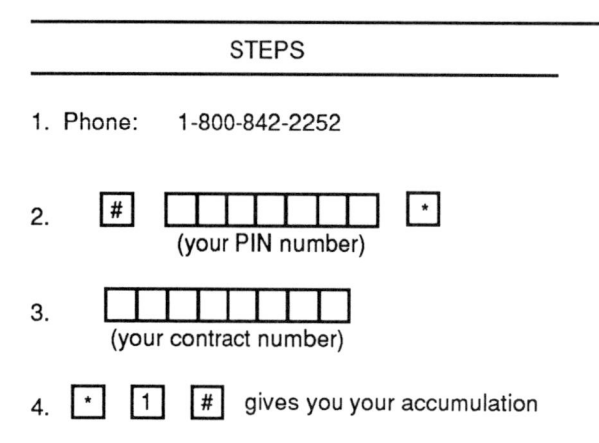

4. [*] [1] [#]   gives you your accumulation

Figure 8.1. Obtaining Your Currrent Annuity Value

By providing one contract number, you will receive the totals for all of your regular annuity accounts. For SRA information, a separate request will have to be made. The system provides the number of units for each contract, and for the CREF funds, the current unit value, as well as the amount you have accumulated. Although the system may be difficult to understand at first, after a few inquiries you will know what to expect and will have no trouble using it.

Making Accumulation Transfers Between Accounts

To make an accumulation transfer means to take funds that are currently in one account and move them to another account. As we have stated numerous times before, making an accumulation transfer has no effect on future allocations of new money going into your TIAA-CREF accounts. To change these allocations, an "Allocation Change" must be made (we'll explain how to do this in the next section). Figure 8.2 provides the fast track system for making transfers between accounts. Before attempting this procedure it is important to keep in mind that transfers can be partial as well as full. Partial transfers must be at least $1,000.

Note that your instructions will be repeated back to you for confirmation, after you've finished. You will also receive written confirmation of the transfer and it will appear again on your next Quarterly Report in the "Summary of Transactions" section.

STEPS

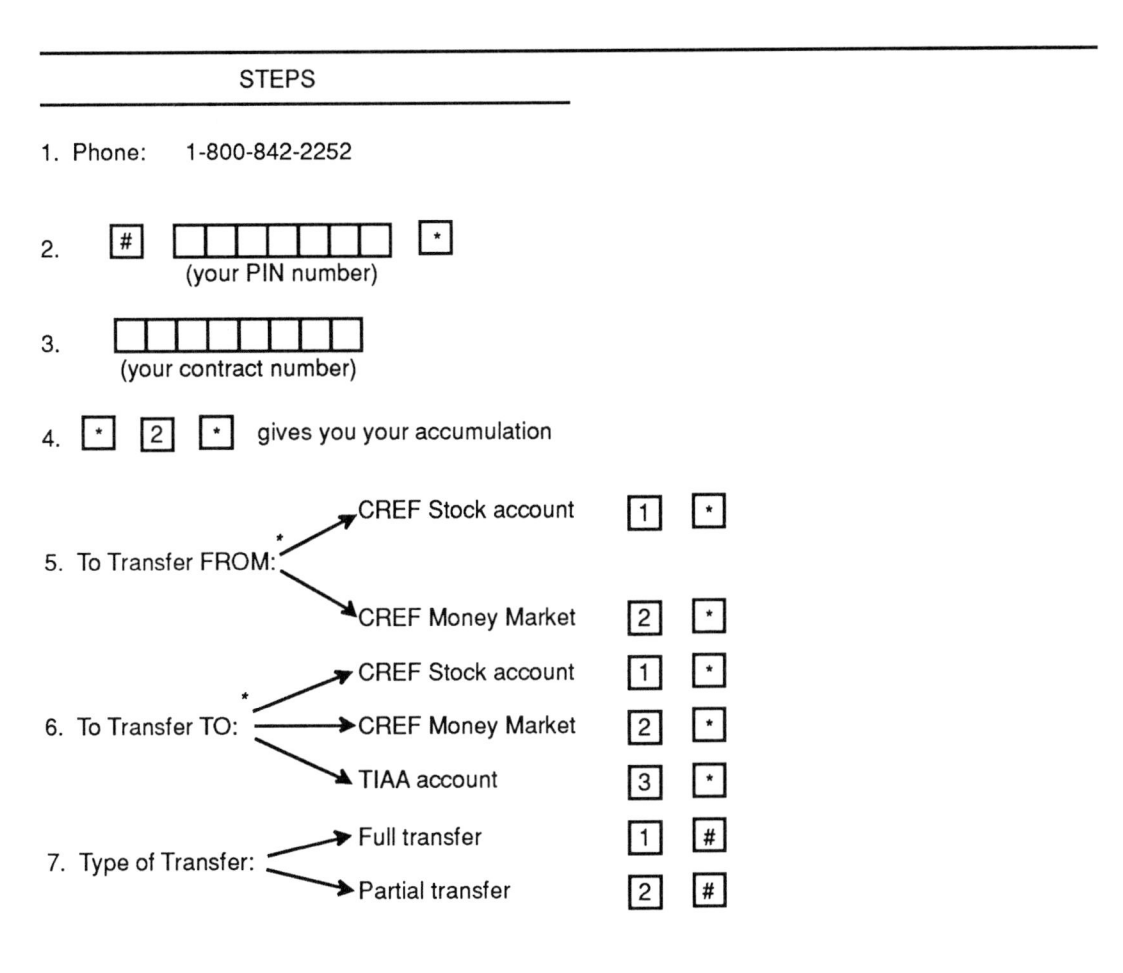

1. Phone: 1-800-842-2252

2. [#] [ ][ ][ ][ ][ ][ ][ ] [*]
   (your PIN number)

3. [ ][ ][ ][ ][ ][ ][ ]
   (your contract number)

4. [*] [2] [*] gives you your accumulation

5. To Transfer FROM:
   - CREF Stock account [1] [*]
   - CREF Money Market [2] [*]

6. To Transfer TO:
   - CREF Stock account [1] [*]
   - CREF Money Market [2] [*]
   - TIAA account [3] [*]

7. Type of Transfer:
   - Full transfer [1] [#]
   - Partial transfer [2] [#]

8. Respond to dialogue

* Note: There will be additional numbers for the new CREF offerings. Reading *The Participant* will keep you informed.

Figure 8.2. Making a Fast-Path Transfer of Accumulated Funds

Making an Allocation Change for Future TIAA-CREF Payments

To affect where your future payments will go, it is necessary to make an allocation change. Figure 8.3 provides the sequence required to make this change. As with transfers, your instructions are confirmed three ways: upon completion of your request, in writing shortly after making the change, and in the next Quarterly Confirmation of Transactions Report.

STEPS

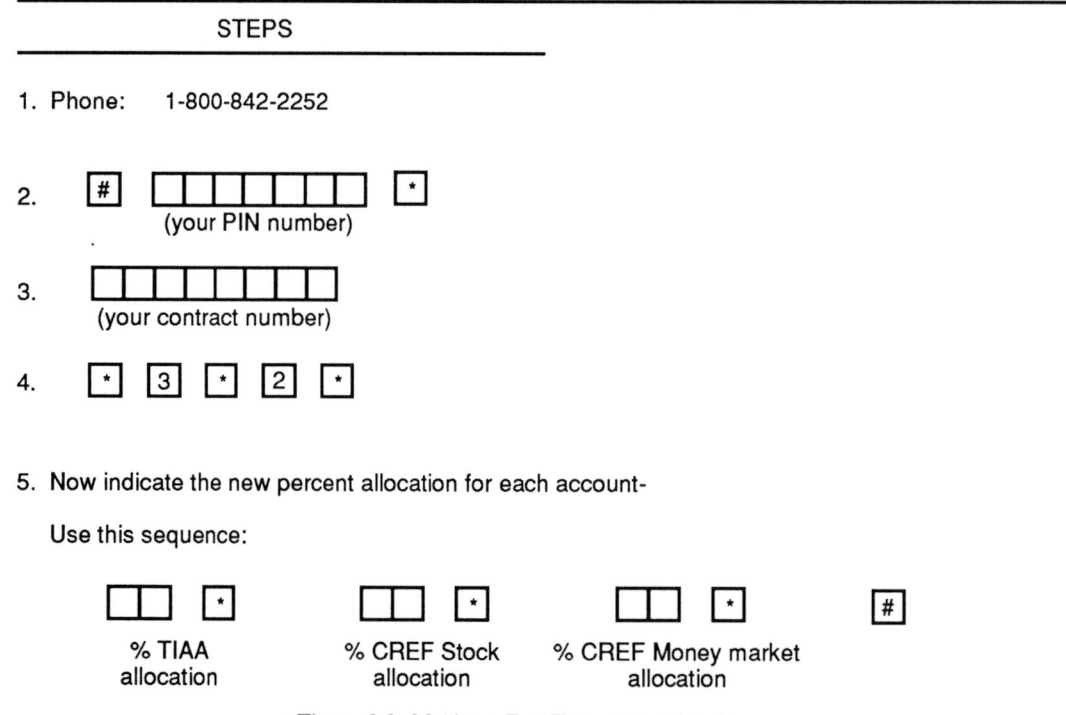

1. Phone: 1-800-842-2252

2. [#] [ ][ ][ ][ ][ ][ ] [*]
   (your PIN number)

3. [ ][ ][ ][ ][ ][ ][ ]
   (your contract number)

4. [*] [3] [*] [2] [*]

5. Now indicate the new percent allocation for each account-

   Use this sequence:

   [ ][ ] [*]   [ ][ ] [*]   [ ][ ] [*]   [#]
   % TIAA   % CREF Stock   % CREF Money market
   allocation   allocation   allocation

   Figure 8.3. Making a Fast-Trace Allocation Change

The Automated Telephone Service allows multiple transactions to be made while on the line. For the first time user, or for a very infrequent user, we suggest that you keep things simple and perform just one task per phone call. After getting accustomed to the system, you may want to perform more than one task during a call. As an example, you can make an accumulation inquiry then make a partial transfer from CREF Stock to CREF Money Market account. To perform multiple tasks, stay on the line after finishing your initial task (for example, getting a quote) and you will be prompted for what you want to do next. You can then proceed using the dialogue or the fast tract "*" system to skip over the dialogue.

Obtaining your Retirement Benefits

TIAA-CREF provides numerous options for receiving benefits under the retirement plan. It is extremely important that you spend time studying all of these options before making a commitment as to how you will take your benefits.

There are three options for receiving money from the retirement plan: 1) lump-sum cash payment, 2) interest-only payments, and 3) contract annuity income. Each of the three options have restrictions, so they have to be examined closely.

Cash Payments

It is currently possible to receive up to 10 percent of TIAA-CREF accumulations in a cash payment upon retirement. If this option is taken, it is important to realize that the money will be removed from its tax-sheltered umbrella, so it will be subject to tax consequences (unless, of course, it is placed into another tax-sheltered account). Not only will the amount be taxed, but if it is reinvested, any interest or capital gains accruing in the future will also be subject to tax. In general then, if you do not need the money for any specific purpose, it is best to leave (or place) it where it will remain free from the tax collector. This advice holds true when considering lump-sum withdrawals from all tax shelters—let the money compound tax-free unless you have a specific use for it.

The lump-sum withdrawal option is undergoing changes at TIAA-CREF, which will benefit some participants. The first change involves the CREF Group Retirement Annuity II. This annuity, which is an option at the institutional level, allows policyholders to transfer their retirement savings from future contributions among the TIAA-CREF accounts and also other non-TIAA-CREF annuities that have been approved by the institution. Moreover, at termination the policyholder is allowed to take the money out in cash, if the institution permits. The bottom line is that the GRA II allows for much greater flexibility for the participant. The limitations on GRA II are that the institution where you make contributions must adopt it, and it is applicable to *new* money only; the flexibility does not apply to previous money accumulated in non-GRA II accounts.

It appears that there may in the future be a way to remove larger lump-sums from your "old money" accounts. TIAA-CREF has proposed the option that would permit policyholders to move present accumulations to non-TIAA-CREF funds and to receive 100 percent cash on termination of employment (subject to individual employer approval). Continued reading of the TIAA-CREF publication *The Participant* will keep you up to date on these and other changes.

One advantage of being able to remove a large lump sum is annual payment control. If the withdrawn money from TIAA-CREF is placed in an IRA, you will be able to retain tax shelter status while being able to withdraw any portion of the funds that you want to each year. If, for example, you should receive a substantial royalty check in a given year, you could choose not to withdraw any money for a period of time, letting the funds compound tax free until you need it (after age 70 1/2, however, there are mandated minimum amounts that must be withdrawn annually). With TIAA-CREF annuities, you will receive a check each month whether you need the money or not.

A second advantage relates to the unisex mortality tables used by TIAA-CREF . A recent court decision requires TIAA-CREF to assume, for the purpose of computing benefit payments, that men and women do not have different average life spans. This has resulted in monthly checks that are smaller than they otherwise would be for men as they are forced to subsidize the payments of longer-living women. Transferring money to an IRA allows do-it-yourself withdrawals which will eliminate this problem. We'll say more about the unisex tables later in the chapter.

The Interest Only Option

A second way to receive annuity benefits is to make use of the new Interest Payment Retirement Option (IPRO). This option allows you to receive interest and dividend payments *only,* while leaving the principal value of the accumulation intact. This allows you to postpone the irrevocable decision on the type of lifetime annuity payment you want until a later date. The advantage of taking this option is that your accumulations can remain unchanged during your early retirement years while you get a good feel for how much money you will need from your TIAA-CREF source to help in supporting your lifestyle. Living in retirement will also provide a much better understanding of the potential impact of the various annuity options on your situation.

Receiving Annuity Income

Upon retirement you receive income by having your TIAA-CREF accumulations purchase annuities. The basic concept of an annuity is the payment of money over a *lifetime.* This means there is no possibility that money will run out before death. With a lifetime income, spending decisions can be made without the fearful prospect of outliving one's supply of money. Because of the many unique situations faced by TIAA-CREF participants at retirement with regard to age, health, dependent needs, other money available, risk tolerance, and so on, TIAA-CREF offers many options for receiving annuity income. Deciding which annuity to purchase at retirement is like purchasing a house. You have many factors to consider and you should get all of your questions answered before making a decision. This decision is so important that, if you are unsure of what to do, you should initially take the interest and dividend option previously discussed. The final annuity decision can then be postponed until you have a full understanding of all the options and how they will impact on your lifestyle.

Annuity income can originate from TIAA annuities or CREF annuities. TIAA lifetime income consists of a monthly guaranteed contractual payment (fixed portion) plus dividends (variable portion). The dividends arise primarily from investment earnings in excess of the guaranteed (fixed portion) rate. These dividends are declared for one year at a time. Because the investments made by TIAA are primarily of a long-term fixed income nature, the declared dividend rate tends to change only gradually.

CREF annuity income comes from either stock market investments, money market (short-term debt) investments, or bond (long-term debt) investments. Monthly CREF income is paid in terms of a fixed number of annuity units. While the number is fixed, their *value* changes based on investment performances. This value change is made once a year (May 1) based on the net total return from investments over the prior twelve months. Because of the volatility of stock prices and rapid changes in interest rates, the CREF stock, bond, and money market accounts can be expected to experience greater variability of returns on an annual basis than that experienced by the TIAA annuity.

Contract Annuity Payment Options

Of the income options available, they can be classified as either "one-life" annuities or "survivor option" annuities. The first question you should ask yourself is which of these two option classifications applies best to your situation.

One-life Options

One-life annuities pay a guaranteed income for the life of one person only. Whether you live for one month or 500 months after choosing this option, the checks will keep coming for your life-time. Because there is no one else for whom TIAA-CREF guarantees to pay lifetime benefits when you die, this option pays you the highest monthly income. For someone without a spouse, child, or significant-other requiring support, this option is the obvious choice.

If a beneficiary is involved, it is possible to obtain *some* protection under the one-life option. By accepting a smaller monthly income, you can insure a benefit for a specified period of time whether you live or not. For example, under a one-life annuity with a 20 year guaranteed period, income will be paid to your beneficiary for up to 20 years should you die at any time prior to the end of the 20 year period. If you continue to live beyond the 20 year period, benefits will keep coming to you until your death—no matter how long that is. The important fact to keep in mind is that payments to the beneficiary under this option are *not* for his or her lifetime—they will stop at the end of the guaranteed period. This means that the spending and lifestyle decisions of the beneficiary may be affected at the end of the guaranteed period and possibly well before it, as the beneficiary may begin to worry over future sources of income as the end of the guaranteed period nears. If a substantial amount of retirement income exists from sources other than TIAA-CREF, this may not be a major concern. However, if the beneficiary is expected to rely heavily on the income for financial support, the choice of this option could have a devastating effect on his or her future life-style, should you die first.

At the present time TIAA-CREF allows a choice of three guaranteed periods under the one-life option: 10, 15 years or 20 years. For most participants having beneficiaries without a lifestyle-maintaining retirement income from another source, the one-life options should be avoided.

A variant of the guaranteed period payment method is the installment refund annuity. With this one-person annuity option, you receive income for life but if you should die before receiving a total amount of annuity payments equal to the full accumulation in your account when payments started, the income continues to your beneficiary until the initial amount is paid out. This option only applies to TIAA annuities paid out under the level payment method. As an example, if an annuitant had $200,000 accrued at the time retirement annuity income commenced, and the annuitant died within the first year of retirement, the entire $200,000 would be paid out to the named beneficiary.

Survivor Options

With Survivor Options, two annuitants are identified, with benefits extending throughout the lives of both individuals. This means that a TIAA-CREF participant under this option is assured that his or her spouse can receive payments for life, no matter how long he or she lives, should the participant die first.

There are three basic income alternatives to choose from in Survivor Options annuities: 1) full benefit to the survivor, 2) two-thirds benefit to the survivor, and 3) half benefit to the survivor. For each of these alternatives, you have a further option to name a beneficiary to receive an income for the balance of a specified time should both annuitants die before the end of that time period. Of course, the greater the potential benefits, the smaller will be your monthly annuity check, as you are in effect buying an "insurance policy" for these additional benefits.

As an example, let's say a husband and wife name their daughter as a beneficiary under the 10 year guarantee period. If they should both die at the end of five years of receiving annuity income, their daughter would receive benefits for the remaining five years of the ten year guarantee period.

If providing money to a beneficiary in the event that both annuitants should die is not applicable for your situation, you can have a Survivor Option without a guaranteed period. This will result in greater monthly income to the annuitants. The guarantee periods available for beneficiaries with this option are 10, 15, and 20 years.

TIAA Payment Methods—Level vs. Graded

There are two ways to receive TIAA annuity income: through a level payment plan (the typical method of payment), or through a graded payment plan. Payments under the graded payment plan start out much lower than under the level plan, but increase as the years go by. The graded payment plan works by using the bulk of dividend interest to buy future annuity income instead of immediately paying it out.

The argument for using the graded payment option is that the increasing payments will tend to protect the annuitant from inflation's negative effect on purchasing power. The "real value" of the annuity will tend to be preserved over the long run by the gradual payment increases. This protection is more important for early retirees and others expecting to receive annuity income for a long period of time after annuity income starts. The downside from this approach is that the initial payments are *substantially* lower. As an example, for a husband and wife annuity with a 20 year guarantee period and full benefits to survivor option, a $100,000 TIAA accumulation, under current rates and dividends would pay out $872 per month under the level payment approach. Under the graded payout method, the payout would only be about $500 per month. For the graded method to catch up with the level method will take over ten years.

In general, you can expect about 40 percent less starting income under the graded option, with about a ten year period of smaller monthly payments. Even when payments "catch up" on a numerical basis after ten years, you are really not even, for under the level method you would have received additional payments from the level method for each month of the prior ten years. Moreover, during that period dollars are eroded by inflation. It can also be argued that in the early years of retirement (for example, ages 65 through 75) the retiree is more likely to be healthy and active than in the later years. Receiving more money early may have a greater positive impact on total lifestyle than withholding it until later.

An effect similar to the graded method can be obtained by "phasing-in" your retirement annuity income. As a TIAA-CREF participant you can choose different starting dates for portions of your TIAA-CREF accumulations, as long as each portion is $10,000 or more. As an example, an annuitant could choose to start receiving income from one-fourth of TIAA accumulations immediately upon retirement, then phase in the rest of adding another one-fourth after each two year period in the future. Postponements allow accumulations to compound tax-free, making a larger total for purchasing an annuity at the time of phase-in. In general, each year's delay of receiving payments after the age of 65 results in a monthly payment of about 10 percent more.

The phase-in option is available for all of the TIAA-CREF accounts. The only restriction is the previously mentioned $10,000 minimum phase-in portion. Participants with post-retirement consulting, royalty or part-time income that is expected to diminish over the years can make good use of the phase-in method. They can use TIAA-CREF annuities to "level" retirement income, with the delay in receiving total annuity income offering the potential for much greater benefits over the remaining life-span.

Getting Help Choosing Benefit Options

With such a wide array of benefit payment options, it can be difficult to make the right choices. TIAA-CREF has a free consulting service that will "walk-you" through the various options. Based on your accumulations and unique situation at retirement, they can help you calculate your approximate retirement income under different options. Even if you think you know just what you want to do, you should make use of this free service to discuss your choices.

As a review of the information in this section, figure 8.4 provides a list of major questions that you should ask yourself during the decision making process.

> 1. Is there anyone other than myself and spouse that *needs* to receive benefits?
> 2. What sources (and amounts) of investment income are available after retirement?
> 3. What will be the amount and timing of income from post-retirement activities?
> 4. What will my retirement lifestyle be like?
> 5. Can I expect any special tax consequences (e.g., money from the sale of a principle residence) after retirement?
> 6. Do I or my second annuitant realistically expect to receive annuity income for a long enough period of time that inflation effects are likely to be of major importance?
> 7. Will I be adversely affected by the unisex ruling?
> 8. Will I have a definite need for a lump sum at retirement?
> 9. Is stability of income more important to me than potentially greater (but more variable) income?
> 10. Do I have a full understanding of benefit options and their likely effect on my retirement lifestyle after retirement?

Figure 8.4. Some Questions to Ask Yourself Before Choosing Annuity Benefits

The Unisex Ruling and Annuity Income

On average, women live longer than men. For many years, companies such as TIAA-CREF, recognizing this fact, used two life expectancy tables to calculate the annuity payments that each sex would receive. Since annuity payments, by definition, last for the lifetime of the individual receiving them, women received a smaller monthly payment than men, to compensate for the expectation that more monthly payments would have to be paid. In 1983 the Supreme Court ruled that this policy was discriminatory. TIAA-CREF and other companies offering defined contribution pension plans now use unisex tables to calculate annuity benefits. Since women live longer than men as a group, it simply means that they will receive more total benefits than men will.

The switch to unisex mortality tables operates to generally reduce monthly payments to men and generally increase monthly payments to women. Of course the type of annuity makes a big difference in the amount of the effect. Since joint-life annuities involve both sexes (the surviving spouse receives lifetime income after the TIAA-CREF participant dies), the change to unisex tables provides little or no change in monthly benefits for users of this option. For single-life annuities, the situation is different. For a man, CREF monthly benefits are lowered by about 8 percent from what they would be if male morality tables were used, and women receive about 8 percent more than they otherwise would if female tables were used. For TIAA annuities, the differences are about 4 1/2 percent.

For a woman using the single-life annuity option, the unisex tables offer a windfall of benefits if she lives in accordance with the expectations of her gender class. For a man, the single-life option suffers in its payments, as total female payment expectations must be subsidized by the male monthly payments. Because the payments are favorable for women, they need to do nothing but accept the situation. Men using the single-life option may want to avoid the adverse effects by taking as much money as possible in cash at retirement and placing it in a tax-sheltered vehicle that is free from the sex bias. An IRA account and many insurance company annuities are possible options. The present maximum of ten percent retirement withdrawal from TIAA-CREF is a distinct limitation to the effectiveness of this practice. Future expectations of a 100 percent withdrawal option will make this approach more effective.

Supplemental Retirement Annuities

A special benefit available to employees of educational institutions is the Tax Sheltered Annuity. The TSA provides a way for educators to save additional money beyond that accumulated in the regular TIAA-CREF retirement annuity program. If you find yourself in the fortunate position of having additional money available each month to be saved for retirement, you should make use of this special program. It is one of the few tax-advantaged perks that educators have available to them today.

Under this law, if the employer contributes to a TSA, the contribution is not taxable. To make use of this benefit, it is necessary to sign a reduction-in-salary agreement so the contributions are being made by the institution. This agreement satisfies the legal requirement that the payments not come from your salary and therefore allows the contributions to have a non-taxable status. Each year the IRS allows only one agreement to be made, so any desired changes (for example, reducing the monthly amount contributed) have to wait until the next calendar year.

Many organizations offer TSA's for educators. The tax sheltered annuity plan run by TIAA-CREF is called their SRA (Supplemental Retirement Annuity) plan. Monthly savings in the SRA can be made into the same TIAA-CREF products that the regular retirement pension accumulations are made into. Transfers between the accounts can be made in accordance with the same rules established for the regular pension. Monthly and annual statements have the same format as the regular TIAA-CREF account, so they are easy for the participant to interpret.

It is surprising how small monthly contributions to a tax sheltered plan can grow to a substantial amount if enough time is involved. Figure 8.5 provides some examples of ending balances for different monthly savings rates over differing periods of time. The message provided by the table is that relatively small amounts saved in a tax sheltered program over a working lifetime can have a significant impact on one's lifestyle in retirement.

Saving $1 a day ($30 a month)

Years	5 percent return	10 percent return
10	$ 4,677	$ 6,195
20	$ 12,381	$ 22,968
30	$ 25,071	$ 68,379
40	$ 45,969	$ 191,301

Saving $10 a day ($300 a month)

Years	5 percent return	10 percent return
10	$ 46,770	$ 61,950
20	$123,810	$ 229,680
30	$250,770	$ 683,790
40	$459,690	$1,913,010

Figure 8.5. Saving Rates and Ending Sums—Example SRA Investment Experience

There is a legal maximum amount that can be contributed each year to a TSA. The multi-part formula for determining this amount is not worth the effort involved in working out yourself, as TIAA-CREF will determine it for you at no charge.

Many options are available for taking money out of the TIAA-CREF SRA. In general, all of the payment options previously discussed for the regular TIAA-CREF retirement plan apply to the SRA, plus there are additional options. One important option is that you can receive the entire accumulation in cash. This means you can rollover the entire amount saved to an IRA, providing the flexibility to choose almost any investment product and any withdrawal method you choose, all under a tax-sheltered umbrella. Also available for the TIAA-CREF SRA are periodic cash payouts over a fixed number of years (between 2 and 30), or partial withdrawals of $1000 or more once a month (or less often, if you prefer).

As you may have guessed, there are penalties on early withdrawals of money from the SRA. This is because the purpose of the tax shelter is to develop retirement savings and not just represent a short-term depository for the accumulation of money. Withdrawals can be made without a 10 percent penalty only if the employee terminates employment, attains the age of 59 1/2, becomes disabled, encounters financial hardship, or dies. For the majority of retirement savers under this plan, these restrictions will not prove to be onerous.

Bibliography

Annual Benefits Report, TIAA-CREF, 1989.

CREF Prospectus and Statement of Additional Information, CREF, 1989.

From Now to Retirement: Planning for Your TIAA-CREF Annuity Benefits, TIAA, 1988.

Quarterly Statement of Transactions and Accumulations, TIAA-CREF, 1989.

The Participant, TIAA, August, 1988; May, 1989.

Understanding Your Annuity Benefits Report, TIAA-CREF, 1989.

Your TIAA and CREF Annuities and the TIAA Graded Benefit Method, TIAA-CREF, 1989.

Chapter 9

Your Other Investments

Up to this point our concern in this book has been with your retirement funds. Many individuals approaching the age of retirement find that the largest single item of their family net worth is the value of their accumulated retirement funds. For the great majority of individuals, however, especially professionals such as those associated with colleges or universities, their retirement funds should not be their *only* invested assets. Good financial planning calls for individuals to have a plan of savings and investments throughout their adult lives.

This chapter is devoted to those investments we hope you are accumulating in addition to your retirement funds. All that can be accomplished in a single chapter is a general overview of the investment opportunities available and a very elementary discussion of how they can fit into your financial and investment planning.

"How much should I save?" That question is commonly addressed to investment advisors, and there is no single right answer. We discussed in Chapter 1 several of the concerns an individual or family must consider in defining their financial needs, but it still is a question that each person must ultimately decide.

One approach suggested by many students of personal finance is what might be called *the 10% solution.* This suggests that a good rule of thumb for many is to attempt to save at least 10% of takehome pay on a regular basis. Some save more, most save less, but this is a reasonable goal for most who have not given much thought to the question.

"There is no way in the world I can do that," is a common response of many who hear this suggestion. At first this may seem an impossible goal. Think for a moment, though, about the many people in the 1980's, those in the airline industry for example, who were afraid their employers were going to go bankrupt and leave them unemployed. In many cases they negotiated new labor contracts that called for salary reductions, often of more than 10%. They found they could live on less when they had to; it was a matter of priorities. How much you are able to save for purposes of investment is to some degree how much you *want* to save.

If you are still absolutely convinced you cannot save 10% even though you would like to, another alternative is *the 50% solution.* In this case an individual decides to place 50% of each salary increase into savings until the goal of 10% of the total is achieved. For example, a person may be saving $70 a month, which is well below their desired 10% goal. If a salary increase results in extra $60 a month of takehome pay, the individual should plan on saving $30 of the new money, thereby giving him a monthly savings of $100. This practice should be continued with each salary increase until the goal of saving 10% has been reached.

University faculty have other alternatives for disciplining themselves to achieve savings goals. Summer school pay can be set aside for savings. A certain portion of income from extra teaching, lecturing, or consulting can be allocated to savings.

It should be noted that it usually takes no discipline to save for retirement. Most universities and colleges have mandatory retirement contributions. The faculty or staff member has no choice about whether to participate. The savings over and above the retirement program often provide the funds that can make a significant difference in lifestyle both before and after retirement. It is here that self-discipline becomes crucial. No one forces you to save. Everyone—friends, creditors, advertisers—bring pressure to spend. The decision to save, and the discipline to stick with the decision, must be accomplished by the individual or couple involved.

The process of systematic saving is sometimes called "paying yourself first." You must pay others on a regular basis, including the mortgage, car payments, utility bills, etc. This slogan implies that, even before you pay others, you should set money aside into savings to pay yourself. An individual who cannot achieve this alone can get help. There are automatic withholding plans, implemented either by the employer's payroll or personnel office or by the bank where one has an account, whereby an amount can be regularly withheld from salary and invested in savings bonds, mutual funds or other investment options. How the saving and investment plan is accomplished is not as important as the fact that *it is accomplished.*

Coordinating Investments

Whatever investment program one has should be carefully coordinated with the individual's retirement program. As TIAA-CREF investments become more diverse through the addition of the new options, it is imperative that investments inside retirement programs complement other investments one may have. Turn back for a moment to Chapter 1 and look at Figure 1.1. Notice that, in the *Investment Assets* section, John and Mary have not yet included their TIAA-CREF accounts among their investments. Let us assume that they have the following amounts in their retirement funds:

CREF	*$14,000*
CREF Bond Fund	*3,000*
CREF Money Market	*2,000*
TIAA	*4,000*

Figure 9.1 is a revision of the *INVESTMENT ASSETS* section of Figure 1.1 with the above balances placed in the proper categories.

Equities		
Growth Fund	$ 8,100	
Internat. Fund	3,200	
100 Sh Gen Mot	4,300	
50 Sh IBM	6,300	
CREF	14,000	
	$35,900	52.6%
Bonds		
Muni Bond Fund	5,300	
CREF Bond Fund	3,000	
	$ 8,300	12.2%
Cash and Cash Equivalents		
Checking Account	$ 2,000	
Certi. of Deposit	8,000	
Life Ins. Cash Val	1,000	
CREF Money Market	2,000	
TIAA	4,000	
	$17,000	24.9%
Real Estate		
Limited Part.	$ 5,000	7.3%
Precious Metals		
Gold Bullion	$ 2,000	2.9%
TOTAL INVESTMENT ASSETS	$68,200	

Figure 9.1. Investment Assets of John and Mary Saver

We have placed CREF in the Equities category because it is a fund of stocks. The CREF Bond Fund obviously goes into the Bonds section and CREF Money Market is placed in the Cash and Cash Equivalents category. We have also placed TIAA in the latter grouping. You may suggest that, since TIAA contains real estate and mortgages among its investments, it should more appropriately be placed in the Real Estate category. We will not argue too strenuously if you prefer to place it there. We place it in the Cash and Cash Equivalents category because of its guaranteed return characteristic. Participants are assured they will receive at least a specific number of dollars from TIAA. CREF returns will fluctuate more depending on the investment results in the stock and bond markets.

The only purpose of preparing a list like Figure 9.1 is to assist the individual in investment planning and analysis. Wherever TIAA is placed, the investor should keep that placement in mind so that it can be taken into consideration in analyzing the data. For example, if a large TIAA balance were placed under Real Estate, it can distort the numbers and make it look like the investor has a higher percentage of investments in real estate than is really the case. That fact would need to be kept in mind as the individual decides where to invest new funds that become available.

We note first in looking at the new figures that our couple now have a total of $68,200 in investment assets rather than the original amount of $45,200 shown in Figure 1.1. Even more important, we see that John and Mary now have 52.6% of their investment assets in equities rather than the original 48.5%. This difference may seem inconsequential, but it is possible they had decided in their financial planning that they did not want more than 50% of their investments in equities, since such investments are somewhat higher in risk than bonds or cash. They will probably not want to purchase any more stocks or stock mutual funds in the immediate future. Since new CREF funds will go into the account each month, they may even decide to move some of their equities investments to one of the other categories. They could do this either by selling some of their holdings which are outside their retirement funds or by calling TIAA-CREF and moving a portion of the CREF accumulations into one of the other TIAA-CREF options. Evaluations concerning the appropriate amounts to allocate to each category should always take into consideration both retirement funds and other investment funds.

Investment Opportunities

Most of the assets the average investor will have in a personal investment portfolio can be classified in one of the five categories found in Figure 9.1: equities, bonds, cash and cash equivalents, real estate and precious metals. You may want to refer back to Figure 1.2 in Chapter 1 to see a comprehensive listing of various types of investment possibilities within each group.

We will briefly consider each of the categories and discuss how they can be used to develop a balanced investment portfolio. We can only provide a general overview here. The individual who is interested in a particular type of investment should read more and carefully examine its pros and cons. Not only should the merits of any particular investment be analyzed but consideration should be given to how it fits into one's total portfolio.

Equities

Equities are a form of investment that represent ownership. *Common stocks* are the most common type of equity investments, and they represent ownership in corporations. A family may be the only owners of a corporation, and they would therefore own 100% of the stock. The stocks of concern to us here are those that are publicly owned, i.e. the shares are traded on a stock exchange or "over-the-counter" so that individual stockholders may buy, own, and sell them. Institutions, such as pension funds, may also own common stocks. The various CREF stock funds own millions of shares of common stock in various publicly traded corporations.

Equity investments offer a comparatively good opportunity for long term profits, but they also offer relatively higher risk than many other investments. Since the holder of common stock is one of the owners of the corporation, the stockholder has the chance to benefit if the company has rising profits but also shares in the company's risk. If the sales of automobiles soar in a given year, General Motors Corporation will enjoy high profits, and they may vote to share those profits with stockholders in the form of dividends. Alternatively, in a period of recession with several years of sagging auto sales, General Motors may suffer losses or at least a decline in earnings. The stockholder might then be hurt not only by reduced dividends but quite possibly also by a sharp drop in the price of the stock. Some stocks may pay no dividends at all because the company keeps its profits to reinvest rather than sharing them with stockholders. In that case, the stockholders hope to profit through an increase in the price of the stock rather than through direct receipt of dividends.

It is absolutely imperative that the individual investor in common stocks be well informed and do some home work before deciding which stocks to buy. Most people are familiar with the names of such well known company stocks as IBM, General Motors, General Electric and Proctor and Gamble, but there are literally thousands of stocks to choose among. Over 2,000 stocks trade just on the New York Stock Exchange, and more are available on other exchanges. Moreover, there are far more stocks available on foreign than on U.S. exchanges.

Does the individual investor have a chance in such a complex world? The answer is yes. A serious, well informed individual investor can perform well over an extended period of time. Many people will find it worthwhile to supplement their TIAA-CREF or other retirement funds with a portfolio that includes common stocks.

The investor should consider a variety of data when deciding what stocks to purchase. There are generally considered to be two basic approaches to research and analysis of common stocks—fundamental analysis and technical analysis. The predominant approach is *fundamental analysis,* which is involved with evaluating the economic conditions of a company and its operating environment. Without going into detail, it is possible to give the flavor of fundamental analysis by suggesting two of the most important figures monitored by fundamental analysts, dividend yield and price to earnings ratios. Figure 9.2 illustrates how stock information is usually presented in daily papers and shows how to find yield, price/earnings and similar information.

52 Week (1) Hi Lo	Stock	Div (2)	Yield% (3)	P/E (4)	Vol(000) (5)	Daily Price Hi Lo	(6) Close	Change (7)
51 1/2 39 1/4	Bell So	2.52	5.7	14	483	45 43 1/2	44 1/4	+1/2
56 1/4 31	Pepsi Co	1.00	1.8	18	279	51 50 3/8	50 1/2	—

Notes
1. Indicates the highest and lowest price at which the stock has sold during the last 52 week period. Note that prices are quoted in fractions of a dollar. 52 1/2 is a price of $52.50; 39 1/4 is $39.25.
2. Shows the dividend paid per share during the past year. Pepsico is shown to be paying $1.00 per share annually. Bell South is paying $2.52.
3. The yield is calculated by dividing the dividend by the closing price. Bell South's dividend of $2.52 is a 5.7% yield on a closing price of $44.25.
4. The price/earnings ratio (P/E) is calculated by dividing the price by the latest 12 months earnings. The earnings are not shown on the chart. The person preparing the chart must have that information available independently.
5. Shows the volume of sales on that particular day. On the day shown, 483,000 shares of Bell South stock was traded; the figure for PepsiCo was 279,000.
6. Shows the highest and lowest price at which a stock traded on that particular day and the last (closing) price at which it traded.
7. Shows the change between today's closing price and yesterday's closing price. Bell South's price was up by $ .50. which tells us that yesterday's closing price was $43.75; PepsiCo's price was unchanged from the previous day.

Figure 9.2. Daily Stock Market Quotations as Found in Major Daily Newspapers

Dividend yield refers to the relationship between the price of a stock and the amount of dividend it pays. A stock selling for $10.00 per share and paying $1.00 per share dividend each year is said to have a dividend yield of 10%. In the real world that would be a relatively high yield. *Barron's,* the weekly financial magazine, regularly publishes historical stock market data which indicates that, over the last half-century, the highest year-end average dividend yield for the market as a whole was 6.85% in 1950 and the lowest was 2.95% in 1965. Just before the stock market crash in October, 1987, the price of stocks had risen so high that stocks on the New York Stock Exchange were paying an average dividend of less than 3%. Note that the return on the two stocks in Figure 8.2 is 5.7% for Bell South, not unusual since utilities tend to pay higher dividends than the market as a whole. PepsiCo was paying only 1.8%, again not unusual since this company tends to reinvest its earnings in the company rather than paying high dividends.

Different individuals will have varying objectives concerning dividends. Those at or near retirement may want to own stocks that pay high current dividends. Younger individuals and those who have sufficient income from other sources may prefer to own stocks which pay low current dividends but have the potential to pay higher dividends or experience a rise in stock price in the future.

Another indicator closely watched by investors is the price/earnings ratio. This shows the price of the stock as it relates to the company's profits, or earnings. A company that is selling for $15.00 a share and having earnings that year of $1.00 per share would have a price/earnings (P/E) ratio of 15/1. That means the investor is willing to pay $15.00 to buy $1.00 of current earning power. There are no quick and easy rules for what constitutes the correct P/E. The *Barron's* data mentioned above show that the highest year-end P/E for New York Stock Exchange stocks was 22.9 in 1961 and the lowest was 6.2 in 1974. In the late 1980's, there was concern about the Tokyo Stock Exchange because many Japanese stocks sold at P/E ratios of 60/1 or more. The P/E ratios of the two stocks in Figure 8.2 are 14 and 18, neither unusually high nor low.

A potential stock buyer should take care to consider what a P/E means. A low P/E may mean that a stock is a good value, or it may be a warning that stock analysts have found something potentially wrong with the stock and are unwilling to pay more for it.

Dividend yields and P/E ratios are just two indicators to be considered with others in reviewing stocks. A student of fundamental analysis would also look at the balance sheet, the record of earnings growth over several years, projected growth in the future, dividend payment growth, etc. It would also be important to make a subjective evaluation about markets, potential competition, the strength of the economy, etc. The Value Line Investment Survey, available by subscription and found in most libraries, provides a wealth of fundamental information on 1500 actively traded stocks.

Fundamental Indicators
    Dividend yield
    Dividend growth rate
    Price to earnings ratio
    Price to sales ratio
    Earnings growth rate
    Profit margin
    Return on equity
    Debt to equity ratio
    Price to book value ratio

Technical Indicators

    Moving averages
    Resistance levels
    Support levels
    Stock momentum
    Sales volume
    Accumulation patterns
    Distribution patterns
    Positive volume
    Negative volume
    Oscillators
    Relative strength indicators

Figure 9.3. Selected Stock Market Indicators

Technical analysis is concerned not so much with the internal condition of a company as with its price movement patterns on the stock exchange. Figure 9.3 shows the comparison of indicators watched by fundamental and technical analysts. Charts have traditionally been the basic tool of the technician. Figure 9.4 is a simple example of what a technical analyst might look for. The technician would note that there is a "support level" at about the price of 8. When the price falls to that level, there are a lot of potential buyers so the price bounces back up. Likewise, there is a "resistance level" at about 11. When the price gets that high, it tends to fall back again. An observer of these price movements might expect that if the stock breaks through either of these points for a period of time it will continue to move in that direction until it establishes another support or resistance level.

Notes: Resistance level at about 11.
Support level at about 8.

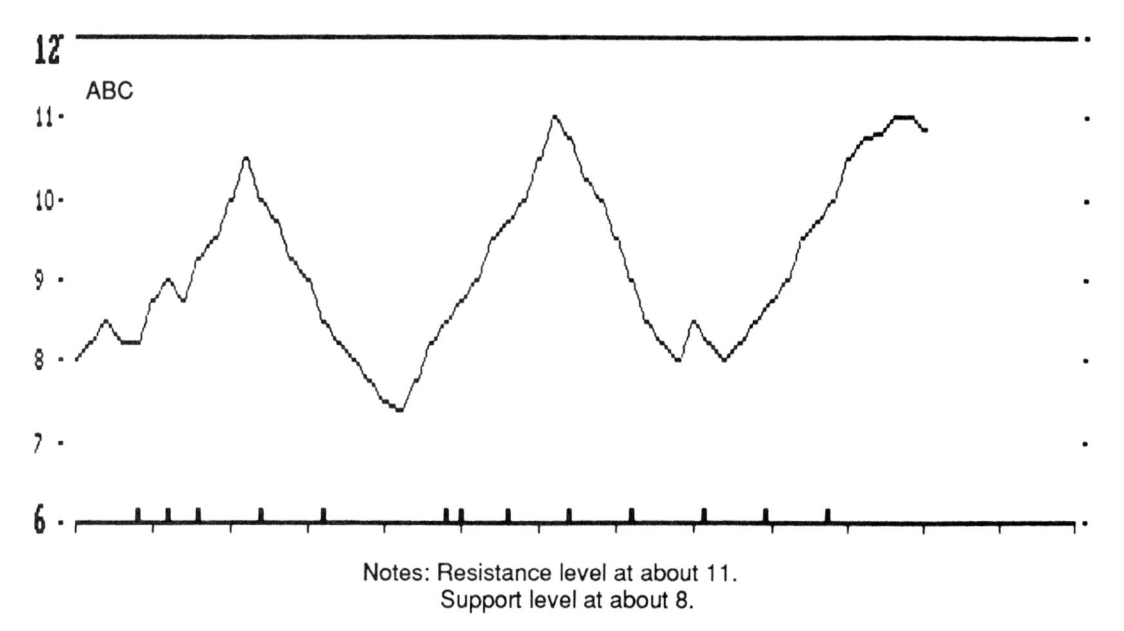

Figure 9.4. Price Movements of Stock of Mythical ABC Company

The volume of sales is also of concern to the technician. High volume is an indication that there is momentum behind the movement of stock price in a given direction. There are many subjects of technical analysis. Technical analysis is more an art than a science, and like fundamental analysis, a considerable amount of subjectivity is built into the evaluation process.

Peter Lynch, the manager of the highly successful Fidelity Magellan Fund and author of a fine investment book, *One Up on Wall Street,* suggests a way to supplement fundamental and technical research. He says the average small investor can be "one up" on the professionals by investing in what he or she knows. The person who works for an auto company may be in the best position to know which companies are doing well and which may face problems in the future. A professor of computer science may have a good feel for which computer companies appear to be bringing the most profitable products to market. The wise investor will make use of the knowledge available through training or professional competence to help in stock selection.

Fundamental and technical analysis both deserve far more attention than the few paragraphs we can devote to them here. *The evaluation and selection of common stocks is serious business.* One does not have to be a broker or full time professional to choose stocks for purchase, but it cannot be a haphazard or "seat of the pants" procedure. The person who buys stocks on the basis of a tip received over lunch or coffee break will probably get burned by the stock purchase if not by the coffee.

The individual who wants to invest in equities without the problems of choosing individual stocks should consider the possibilities of investing in *mutual funds*. Mutual funds pool investors' money to invest in securities. They provide the individual with several advantages, the most important of which is probably diversification. A person who invests in a mutual fund is actually an owner of each of the individual companies owned by the fund no matter how small his or her investment might be. By buying shares in a mutual fund an investor achieves a degree of diversification that would be virtually impossible for an individual to achieve in one's own personal portfolio.

The CREF stock funds operate much like stock mutual funds. They invest in many different stocks, providing participants with wide diversification. Such funds may provide general diversification, or they may diversify within certain specific guidelines. The CREF International Equities fund, for example, is designed to concentrate on stocks of other countries. The CREF funds are retirement funds, of course, and cannot be purchased for regular investment accounts.

Mutual funds also provide for professional management. They can hire a staff of investment managers, stock researchers and economists to apply their expertise to deciding what holdings should be in the fund's portfolio. In addition, they benefit from economies of scale. As the funds grow, they can get lower brokerage rates and spread their management, research and advertising costs over a large number of individuals.

The most common mutual funds are those called *open-end* mutual funds. This means there is no fixed number of mutual fund shares, and the investor buys shares directly from the fund rather than on a stock market. Likewise, an individual wishing to sell shares would sell them back to the fund rather than through a public market. *Closed-end* funds do trade on a market and would be bought and sold through a broker in the same way as individual common stocks.

A buyer of open-end mutual funds must choose between two types: load funds and no-load funds. A load is a sales charge, and a *load-fund* is one which is sold with a sales charge attached. For example, if an individual invested $1,000 in a fund with a 4% load, only $960 would actually get invested on behalf of the investor. The other $40 (4%) would be the load and would go to whoever assisted in the sale of the fund. Funds may also have "back-end loads" or "go-loads" which are charges imposed at the time of sale, rather than purchase, of the fund.

Purchasers of no-load funds do not have to pay such a charge, but they must do a bit more work themselves since the fund has no sales force. They must check out the information, decide which funds to buy, and then send their application and money directly to the fund's office. This is not really a complicated process. Newspapers and financial magazines are full of mutual fund advertisements, most with 800 phone numbers. Individuals may call and have information sent to them on funds in which they think they may have an interest. They can also consult independent information available at most libraries to see which funds have done well in the past.

The available research strongly indicates that there is no discernible difference in the long term investment performance of load and no-load funds. There is no reason why there should be. Remember, the load, or sales charge, does not go to pay for superior management or research services; it goes to pay salesmen.

Most campuses today are visited by salespersons representing load mutual funds for investment in retirement programs such as tax-sheltered annuities (TSA's), individual retirement accounts (IRA's) and supplemental retirement accounts (SRA's) as well as for direct investment in one's personal portfolio. Most are honest and competent and provide a legitimate service. If you feel you need the counseling and assistance they can provide, you may be willing to pay the load associated with their products. *You should ask them to explain clearly all the charges associated with their funds.* Many individuals will prefer to do their own research and home work and purchase no-load funds, thereby avoiding the 2%–8% charges which accompany load funds. As with common stocks, the choice of mutual funds should come only after careful evaluation and analysis of the alternative available.

There are literally thousands of mutual funds available, more funds than there are stocks which trade on the New York Stock Exchange. The following are just a very few examples of open-end stock mutual funds offered by some of the largest investment companies:

	Phone 1–800–
Dreyfus Fund	*645-6561*
Fidelity Magellan	*544-6666*
Financial Dynamics	*525–8085*
Scudder Capital Growth	*225-2470*
Twentieth Century Select	*345–2021*

These are not recommendations. These funds may be good investments at some times and less desirable at others. They are typical of the thousands of funds now available.

Closed-end funds which, as noted, trade on the stock exchanges, would include the following:

>   *Blue Chip Value*
>   *Gemini II Capital*
>   *Korea Fund*
>   *Source Capital*
>   *Zweig*

No phone numbers are provided because these funds are purchased not from the investment company but through your broker. Closed-end funds are not as numerous as open-end ones, but there are still dozens to choose from.

Bonds

Bonds represent a form of *loan*, in contrast to equities, discussed above, which represent ownership. The person who owns a U.S. savings bond or treasury bill has made a loan to the U.S. government, and the government has promised to pay a given rate of interest and to repay the principal of the loan on a given future date. Similarly, a corporate bond represents a loan to a corporation.

Bonds of governmental units and financially stable corporations tend to be very safe investments. They enable the investor to project exactly what the interest income from the bond will be and to know a specific date on which the principal (face amount) of the bond will be repaid. A typical corporate bond might be identified as follows:

>   *General Electric 7 1/2 93*

This means that the bond is issued by General Electric Corp., pays 7.5% interest annually, and the principal will be repaid to the bond holder in 1993. The holder of $10,000 of these bonds will receive $750 per year (7.5%) in interest income.

Bondholders do not share in the profits of companies. If the profits of General Electric triple, the company will still owe the bondholder $10,000. In contrast, the General Electric stockholder might expect to see dividends rise and the price of the stock increase if profits increase dramatically. The stockholder must also accept the risk of lower profits and perhaps lower dividends and stock price for a while. Bondholders do not face these risks; they have a right to the interest and face value of the bond and can expect to receive them unless the company actually goes bankrupt.

For these reasons high grade bonds tend to be viewed as a safer and more stable investment than stocks. A conservative, risk-averse investor might want proportionately more of his or her portfolio in bonds than would a more aggressive investor. This is not to imply that bonds have *no* risk. Bondholders face the risk of inflation. While the owner of the bond mentioned above knows he will receive exactly $10,000 in 1993, there is no way of knowing what that amount will buy in 1993. If the annual inflation rate is 9% and the bond is paying only 7.5%, the bondholder is in the unfortunate position of getting a *negative return* on that investment.

Bonds also fluctuate in price. While we know our General Electric bond will repay the face value of $10,000 in 1993, it may at various times be worth either more or less than that between now and the maturity date. Bonds fluctuate in price in inverse relationship to interest rates; when interest rates rise, the price of bonds declines and vice versa. Bond investors should keep this possible fluctuation in consideration since it can affect the rate of return received. In recent years some companies have issued high risk, high yield bonds, sometimes called "junk bonds." Potential buyers should recognize that such bonds carry an unusual level of risk and are often better considered speculations than investments.

Certain types of bonds, called municipal bonds, have the additional advantage of providing tax-exempt income. The holders of municipal bonds—issued by cities, counties, states, school districts, etc.—do not have to pay federal income tax on their interest income from such bonds (though they may have to pay state income tax). This can be a significant saving, as Figure 9.5 indicates.

EQUIVALENT TAX-FREE YIELD

Tax Bracket	6%	8%	10%	12%	14%
15%	7.06	9.41	11.76	14.12	16.47
28%	8.33	11.11	13.89	16.67	19.44
33%	8.96	11.94	14.92	17.91	20.00

Figure 9.5. Taxable Equivlent Yields

For example, the person in the 33% tax bracket would have to get 11.94% return on a taxable bond to be equal to an 8% return on a tax-free municipal bond. If an individual has tax-exempt bonds in a personal portfolio, they should definitely be in that part of the portfolio which is not part of retirement funds. Retirement funds are already tax-sheltered. There is no purpose in putting municipal bonds in a retirement fund since these bonds are already protected from having to pay current income taxes.

Bonds are commonly sold through brokers in units of $10,000 or more, making them rather expensive for many individual investors. As with common stocks, bonds can also be purchased in the form of mutual funds, where the minimum purchase is often much less. The CREF Bond fund has the characteristics of a bond mutual fund. Note in Figure 9.1 that John and Mary own some of the CREF bond fund and also own a municipal bond mutual fund as part of their regular portfolio.

Most bond mutual funds have one characteristic which is fundamentally different from individual bonds. They have no maturity date. Since the fund consists of many different bonds, there is no one date on which they all mature. The mutual fund investor cannot, therefore, be sure of a future date when the amount invested can be retrieved. Bond funds, like individual bonds, will fluctuate in price, and when the investor wants his money back, the price may be either more or less than the price originally paid. There are certain bond funds which are structured so as to have a specific maturity date, but most do not. The investor should be aware of these characteristics when deciding which bond or bond fund to buy.

The following would be examples of mutual funds which invest primarily in high grade bonds:

	Phone 1–800–
AARP General Bond	*253–2277*
Dreyfus A Bonds Plus	*645–6561*
Financial Select Income	*525–8085*
Scudder Income Fund	*225–2470*
Strong Short Term Bond	*368–3863*

Funds which invest only in U.S. government bonds and other securities issued by the government would be considered among the safest of funds. Because of this safety they will pay somewhat lower interest rates than other funds. Examples of funds with portfolios consisting mainly of government securities would include:

	Phone 1–800–
Bull and Bear U.S. Govt. Securities	*847–4200*
Capital Preservation Treas. Note Trust	*227–8380*
Financial U.S. Government Bond	*525–8085*
Twentieth Century U.S. Government	*345–2021*
Vanguard U.S. Treasury Bond	*662–7447*

Examples of tax-free municipal bonds, which offer exemption from the federal income tax, would include the following:

	Phone 1–800–
Dreyfus Tax Exempt	*645–6561*
Fidelity Short Term Tax Free	*544–6666*
T. Rowe Price Tax Free Income	*638–5660*
Safeco Municipal Bond	*426–6730*
Strong Municipal Bond	*368–3863*

Some investment companies offer municipal bond funds which, in addition to being exempt from the federal income tax, are also exempt from state income tax in specific states. If you live in a state with a high state income tax, check with your broker or watch for ads in local papers announcing such funds in your state.

Bonds are an appropriate investment for the person who wants high current income with less risk than is characteristic of stocks. Individuals in high tax brackets will want to give special consideration to municipal bonds. In addition, investors in stocks or stock mutual funds may want to have an amount invested in bonds or bond funds to provide portfolio diversification. A bond investor will need more information than we have space to provide here. Readings in the bibliography will provide needed information on such subjects as callable bonds, "junk bonds," and yield-to-maturity, topics on which one should have some knowledge before making bond investments.

Cash and Cash Equivalents

For many people cash and cash equivalents are the foundation of their investments. After a checking account, they open a savings account and perhaps some certificates of deposit. Such items play a very legitimate role in any investment portfolio. The term, *cash,* should be well understood. It should be noted, however, that cash refers to money held in the currency of one's own country. You may have an envelope full of Swiss francs or German marks. Those are sound currencies, but since one's cash holdings are intended to provide the highest level of security, they are not really a basis for this category. Foreign currencies have the obvious risk of fluctuation in value against the dollar, not a characteristic one wants in cash holdings.

Cash equivalents include such investments as certificates of deposit, money market funds and short-term treasury bills. After the savings and loan problems of the late 1980's, common sense tells us that reasonable care should be taken in deciding where to purchase a certificate of deposit (CD). So long as such care is exercised CD's are a safe way to earn interest on money with minimal risk.

Money market funds are a type of mutual fund which invests in very short term debt securities. They have the advantages of carrying very little risk and have virtually no fluctuation in price. Interest rates on money market funds move up and down quite rapidly since the investments held by the fund are short term and turn over rapidly. Many money market funds allow checks to be written on them, so they can serve as a partial substitute for a checking account. They are a convenient place to "park" investment money and draw interest on it while one is deciding where to invest it for a longer period. The CREF Money Market fund can be used in that way while you are deciding where to invest your retirement funds. Also you will remember that several of our strategies in Chapters 4 through 7 make use of this fund.

Many investment companies which offer stock and bond mutual funds also manage a money market fund. The following would be examples:

	Phone 1–800–
Bull and Bear Dollar Reserves	*847–4200*
Dreyfus Liquid Assets	*645–6561*
Legg Mason Cash Reserves	*822–5544*
T. Rowe Price Prime Reserves	*638–5660*
Twentieth Century Cash Reserve	*345–2021*

Treasury bills, issued by the U.S. government to mature in one year or less, are considered to be among the safest of investments and virtually as safe as money itself. They have the additional advantage of paying a modest rate of interest, which will vary depending on general interest rate levels at any given time. Treasury bills can be purchased from a broker for a minimal fee, or they can be bought directly from any Federal Reserve Bank.

Cash and cash equivalent investments provide the individual with security and liquidity. We discussed in Chapter 1 the need for an emergency fund of from 2 to 6 months living expenses. This does not mean that the money in the investment fund should not be "working" for the investor by earning interest. It just means that such an amount of money should be available on very short notice if needed. Funds in the cash and cash equivalent category should meet this need.

While cash and cash equivalents are considered to be very safe, they do present the investor with inflation risk. One cannot be sure what a specific amount of cash or a money market fund balance will buy at some point in the future. There is also a certain amount of interest rate risk if one gets "locked into" low rates. If one buys an 8 year CD paying 6% and rates later go up to 8% or 9%, the investor is losing interest income. The only way to get the higher rate is to cash in the 8 year CD, and this will probably involve paying a penalty for early withdrawal. This is a good reason to keep such investments in fairly short maturities.

Real Estate

The largest single expenditure most people make during their lifetime is in real estate, the purchase of a home. A home, however, is not an investment asset for most people. It is purchased primarily to satisfy the personal preferences of the individual buying it, and it is unlikely to be sold just because someone comes along and offers a higher price for it. History shows that homes have typically increased in value, and that is a nice benefit for the homeowner, but it is not the main reason most of us want to own our homes.

For many people home ownership is a kind of "forced savings." Individuals who do not discipline themselves to save will, nevertheless, make their monthly mortgage payments. Over a period of time, they will build up equity ownership in the home, and that will increase their net worth. If the value of the home also rises, that will increase net worth even more.

Real estate, as an investment, refers to those real estate holdings we own because we expect to earn a return on our money, either in the form of current income, price appreciation, or in some cases, tax benefits. One can invest in real estate directly, with a "hands-on" approach, or indirectly, through passive ownership.

Active real estate investment requires a special kind of person. The owner of single family homes, apartment houses, or commercial real estate, who also manages the property personally, must know how to select tenants, control costs, manage maintenance programs and perform a variety of other tasks. If the individual is not personally a combined carpenter, plumber, electrician and jack-of-all-trades, he or she must be able to select such specialists and insure that they perform satisfactorily. The alternative is to hire a comprehensive property manager. This step can cut into profits, but it may be appropriate for the investor who cannot, or prefers not, to manage the property personally.

A major advantage of real estate ownership is *leverage,* i.e., the ability to purchase a piece of real estate with a down payment representing only a small fraction of the total value. A property worth $100,000 might be bought with a down payment of only $15,000 or $20,000, and that is just not possible with most other kinds of investments. On the other hand, a low down payment necessitates paying off a large mortgage, and that can place a heavy burden on the owner. It is often impossible to get rental payments high enough to cover mortgage costs.

Owners of investment real estate have also benefitted from the long term trend of rising values. Real estate investors should be aware that the increase in value is not always a straight line movement, as owners of midwestern farm land or residential property in Houston are painfully aware. Over the long term, however, real estate values have increased at a rate well above the national inflation rate.

Real estate investors have also been able to take advantage of several tax benefits, although there are fewer of these than was true a few years ago. Throughout much of the 1970's and 1980's, real estate owners were able to depreciate their property rapidly, an action that was very helpful in reducing current tax liability, and there were a variety of other tax benefits in owning real estate. Today most of those special benefits no longer exist, but a taxpayer can still deduct interest payments on the mortgage of a home and even a second home (which may in fact be held partially for investment purposes). There is little current incentive, however, to own investment real estate just for tax purposes. An individual should be sure the real estate is a good investment from an economic and financial viewpoint, not just on the basis of taxes, before proceeding with a purchase.

For the investor who does not want to be directly involved in real estate management, but who believes real estate should be part of a balanced, diversified portfolio, there are several ways to invest. As with stocks and bonds, there are *open-end real estate mutual funds* which can be purchased directly from mutual fund companies. Such funds may own all kinds of real estate or they may specialize in residential, commercial or even international real estate.

Real estate investment trusts (REIT's) function very much like closed-end funds. They trade on the stock exchanges and can be purchased or sold through a regular stock broker. Some REIT's own real estate and pass their rental income through directly to the investors in the REIT. Others own mortgages, rather than owning real estate directly, and they pass their income from mortgage payments through to the owners. REIT's suffered from a sharp decline in price in the 1970's when inflation hit builders and lenders very hard. Another form of ownership is through the *real estate limited partnership.* As with the other ownership forms, partnerships pool the money of a group of investors and use it to buy a portfolio of real estate holdings. Like REIT's, they are structured so as not to be incorporated, thereby not being liable for the corporate income tax. They must pass their profits directly through to the owners. In the past many real estate investment programs were designed primarily on the basis of tax planning. Partnerships, especially those which invested heavily in the energy regions of the southwest, have not performed well for their investors in the 1980's. Today nearly all such programs, whether mutual funds, REIT's, or partnerships, are planned to provide current income first and, hopefully, capital gains over several years, with tax concerns being only a minor consideration.

A major disadvantage of most real estate investments, either real estate itself or other indirect forms of ownership, is illiquidity. If you need money quickly, or if you desire to reallocate resources among the various categories of investment assets, it is not always easy to sell real estate in order to do so. Certain real estate mutual funds do the best job of providing liquidity to their investors, but real estate is generally less liquid than most other investments.

There is no real estate fund as such available among the TIAA-CREF offerings, but TIAA's portfolio has very large holdings in real estate and mortgages. When real estate investments do well over a fairly long period of time, it enhances TIAA's ability to provide income appreciably above the level guaranteed to participants.

The number of real estate mutual funds is comparatively small, but three which are offered by large investment companies would be:

	Phone 1–800–
Evergreen Global Real Estate Equity	*235–0064*
T. Rowe Price Realty Income	*638–5660*
U.S. Real Estate	*873–8637*

Real estate investment trusts and real estate limited partnerships are purchased through brokers or financial institutions. There are also some limited partnerships which are organized on a local basis to own real estate in a given community.

Precious Metals

Precious metals, especially gold, evoke strong emotions among many investors. The expression, "as good as gold," indicates the high value which many place on this investment. Remember from Chapter 4 that Harry Browne believes 25% of one's permanent portfolio should be in gold. Throughout most of recorded history, gold has been viewed as a substance with great intrinsic value and has been considered to be the foundation of monetary systems. Particularly in times of rapid inflation and political instability, many people have wanted to invest a portion of their assets in gold.

Your authors are not "gold bugs." We do not advocate large investments in precious metals for most people. We do believe it is appropriate for some people to have a small portion of their investments in precious metals for purposes of achieving portfolio balance and diversification.

Precious metal investments include silver, platinum, and palladium as well as gold. In addition to their intrinsic value, the metals may have specific uses—gold in jewelry, silver in photography, etc.

The investor who wants to include precious metals in a portfolio has several alternatives. One may actually own gold in the form of gold bullion or gold coins. Certain gold coins get their value almost entirely from their gold content, including the American Eagle, Canadian Maple Leaf, and South African Krugerrand, the latter being difficult to obtain the U.S. In addition, the American Eagle coins, which are minted by the U.S. Treasury, are the only gold coin or bullion investment which can legally be held in an individual retirement account.

Numismatic coins are those which are held by collectors, and which get most of their value from their scarcity or historic significance rather than from their bullion content. Investors who hold numismatic coins should be aware that the coins' fluctuation in price level will usually be independent of the price of precious metals.

Investors who prefer not to own coins or bullion have other choices. Some investment firms sell bullion certificates. These are similar to certificates of deposit except that, instead of certifying that the investor has a certain number of dollars on deposit, they certify that the individual has a certain number of ounces of the precious metal on deposit. This eliminates the need for the investor to have a safe, safety deposit box or other storage facility.

Investors may also purchase precious metals mutual funds. There are a few funds which invest directly in bullion, sometimes in the bullion of different precious metals, and other funds invest in companies which mine and process metals. For example, there are funds that concentrate on investing in either North American, South African, or Australian gold mines. Others have a diversified holding of gold mines from different parts of the world.

The "purist" in precious metals investing would say that the person who wants to own precious metals should not buy a mutual fund that owns mining companies. Such funds, they would point out, are stock funds, rather than metals funds, and their price may reflect the quality of management, current profit levels and other factors rather than the price of the precious metal itself.

Precious metals have the disadvantage of providing no current income, although mutual funds of mining companies may pay current dividends. It is possible that there may be price appreciation. Gold increased in price from $35 in 1970 to over $850 in 1980, but it has declined significantly from that high level. Silver went from a price of less than $2 to over $30, but the Hunt brothers of Texas were later accused of attempting to manipulate the silver market and push the price to artificially high levels. Silver has since declined to as low as less than $5, and has sold most of the time in recent years at prices less than $10.

At least since 1980, precious metals have not provided protection against inflation. There has been little evidence in recent years that gold (or the other metals, for that matter) has gone up in times of political instability or unusually high inflation. Supporters of gold investments would probably argue that gold is a better protection against inflation in times of drastic runaway inflation than in times of the moderate, consistent price increases which characterized the 1980's.

If you are interested in precious metals mutual funds, you will need to decide which kind of fund you prefer. In the following list, the first fund invests only in gold bullion and gold coins, and the others invest in mining companies.

	Phone 1–800–
U.S. Gold Trust	*531–5142*
Bull and Bear Gold Investors	*847–4200*
Fidelity Precious Metals & Minerals	*544–6666*
Financial Strategic Gold	*525–8085*
Vanguard Gold and Precious Metals	*662–7447*

Choosing to invest in precious metals is a highly individualistic decision. Some believe such investments to be the best protection against natural, political or economic disasters. Others choose to have no precious metals at all in their portfolios. Each investor should study the issue, read material on the subject, and discuss it with informed colleagues if possible before making a decision.

There is no TIAA-CREF fund that has a policy of investing in precious metals on a regular basis. The investor who wants to own precious metals should plan on owning them as part of a regular investment portfolio rather than as part of retirement funds. The main exception to this, as mentioned above, would be the possibility of placing American Eagles in an IRA.

Using Your Savings in Retirement

The main purpose of a savings and investment program during your working years is to meet your primary financial goals. At different times in your life, these goals may include buying a home, educating your children, or starting a business. A major goal for nearly everyone should be providing for retirement. As you approach your retirement, therefore, you will need to consider the most effective use of your financial resources.

Your investments will supplement your other retirement funds. If you have spent your career in higher education, it is likely that you will receive retirement income from TIAA-CREF or some similar organization. You will probably also receive Social Security and perhaps some other payments such as a military or state government pension.

Upon retirement, one of your first considerations should be the likely effect of inflation on your income during your retirement years. The person who retires at 55 should obviously be more concerned about this than the one who retires at 70. It is a matter that can affect almost every retiree, however, because inflation's impact will be felt after only a few years. Figure 9.6 shows how significant this can be. If inflation is 5% annually (and it has often been above that it the past two decades), an item that costs $1,000 when you retire will cost over $1,600 ten years later. At an 8% inflation rate, prices would more than double in ten years.

You may want to structure your withdrawals from investment funds so that you can have an increasing income as years pass. Chapter 8 discusses ways of doing this with your retirement funds, and similar strategies can be used for your other money as well.

It is also possible to determine how far your investment funds will go after you retire. Figure 9.7 provides the information needed to make this determination. Let us assume you have investments of $127,000 which you want to use during retirement. You want to be assured of an income for 20 years, and you believe you can earn 8% on the money. Using Figure 9.7, go down the 8% column to the point where it intersects with 20 years. You find that every $1,000 will provide you a monthly income of $8.19. Since you have $127,000, multiply the 8.19 by 127, and you find that your monthly income will be $1,040.

In Chapter 8 we discussed the concept of your TIAA-CREF funds providing you an annuity during retirement. This gives you the opportunity to guarantee yourself retirement income for as long as you live. Unless you

Inflation Rate	Current Cost	Cost in 5 Years	Cost in 10 Years	Cost in 20 Years	Cost in 30 Years
5%	$1,000	$1,276	$1,630	$2,653	$ 4,321
8%	1,000	1,469	2,159	4,661	10,063
10%	1,000	1,611	2,594	6,727	17,449
12%	1,000	1,762	3,106	9,646	29,960

Figure 9.6. Inflation's Impact on Living Costs

ANNUAL INTEREST RATE, MONTHLY COMPOUNDING

		4%	6%	8%	10%	12%	14%	16%	18%
	1	$85.12	$85.99	$86.86	$87.72	$88.56	$89.40	$90.23	$91.05
	2	43.39	44.25	45.10	45.95	46.79	47.62	48.46	49.28
	3	29.49	30.35	31.21	32.07	32.92	33.78	34.63	35.49
	4	22.55	23.41	24.28	25.16	26.03	26.91	27.80	28.68
	5	18.38	19.26	20.14	21.04	21.94	22.84	23.76	24.67
	6	16.61	16.50	17.40	18.31	19.22	20.17	21.11	22.06
Years to Depletion	7	13.64	14.53	15.45	16.38	17.33	18.29	19.26	20.24
	8	12.16	13.06	14.00	14.95	15.92	16.91	17.91	18.92
	9	11.01	11.93	12.87	13.85	14.84	15.85	16.89	17.93
	10	10.09	11.02	11.99	12.98	13.99	15.03	16.09	17.17
	11	9.34	10.29	11.27	12.28	13.32	14.38	15.47	16.57
	12	8.72	9.68	10.67	11.70	12.77	13.85	14.97	16.10
	13	8.20	9.16	10.18	11.23	12.31	13.42	14.56	15.72
	14	7.75	8.73	9.76	10.82	11.93	13.07	14.23	15.41
	15	7.36	8.35	9.40	10.48	11.61	12.77	13.95	15.15
	16	7.02	8.03	9.09	10.19	11.33	12.52	13.72	14.95
	17	6.73	7.74	8.82	9.94	11.11	12.31	13.53	14.77
	18	6.47	7.49	8.58	9.72	10.91	12.13	13.37	14.63
	19	6.23	7.27	8.37	9.53	10.74	11.97	13.23	14.51
	20	$6.02	$7.07	$8.19	$9.37	$10.59	$11.84	$13.12	$14.41

Example 1—You have $85,500 drawing 12% interest. You want to withdraw it monthly for 18 years. How much can you withdraw per month?

Go down the 12% column to 18 years, and you will find the figure, 10.91. $1,000 will provide you $10.91 per month for 18 years. Since you have $85,500 invested, multiply the 10.91 by 85.5. Your monthly withdrawals for 18 years will be $932.80.

Example 2—You can earn 10% interest, and you want to withdraw $1,300 a month for 15 years. How much do you need to have invested when you begin your retirement program?

Go down the 10% column to 15 years, and you will find the figure, 10.48. $1,000 will provide you $10.48 per month for 15 years. Since you want $1,300 monthly, divide the 10.48 into 1,300. You will need to invest about $124,000 to assure monthly withdrawals of $1,300.

Figure 9.7. Monthly Withdrawals to Deplete a $1,000 Fund

take your investment funds and purchase an annuity at the time of retirement, there will be considerable uncertainty built into the assumptions about your investment funds. In the example above, we assumed an 8% return for 20 years. They were just that—assumptions. In the real world you cannot be sure, in most cases, what your investments will be earning a decade or more in the future. You also cannot know whether you will live one year or thirty years after you retire.

Life is full of uncertainties, and retirement is no exception. A systematic approach to saving and investing throughout your adult working years is a good way to minimize the possible negative impact of those uncertainties on your retirement years. For most of us no one program will enable us to meet our retirement goals. Social Security alone certainly will not provide us with a comfortable retirement, although it can be an important base. Our retirement fund also may not be sufficient to give us the lifestyle to which we aspire. It is the combination of Social Security, our retirement programs, and our investment funds that will enable us to build a secure future.

Summary

Our purpose in this chapter is to emphasize the importance of having a savings and investment program as well as a retirement program throughout one's adult working years. It is also imperative that the two be coordinated. Most investments fall into one of five categories: equities, bonds, cash and cash equivalents, real estate, and precious metals. Most people with a systematic investment program will invest in at least the first three of these categories.

Some people with a special interest in real estate will choose to own and manage property as part of their total investment portfolio. Others, as the total value of their portfolio grows, will want to add real estate to their holdings in order to maintain diversification. If they have no interest in real estate management, they can use real estate mutual funds, real estate investment trusts or limited partnerships. Real estate must be considered a long term investment because of its illiquid nature.

Precious metals are an appropriate investment for certain investors. Gold, in particular, is considered by many to be a favorite investment for protection against inflation and political instability. Of the five categories of investment assets, this one is likely to be used by somewhat fewer investors than the others. Those with very large portfolios, however, should consider owning precious metals for purposes of portfolio balance and investor safety.

There are other investments besides those we have discussed. Most would be much more speculative, such as commodities, options, foreign currencies, futures, etc. For the average person, these will be of little or no significance to their investment practices. Money devoted to such items should be considered speculations more than investments, and the investor should recognize the very real possibility of losing *all* of the money so invested.

We have provided examples of the types of funds that are found in each category. These are provided to give you a better understanding of various investment opportunities. They are not specific recommendations of the funds listed.

The first three categories—equities, bonds, and cash and cash equivalents—are well represented in the investment alternatives made available by TIAA-CREF. There are ample opportunities to make these types of investments either inside one's retirement funds or through one's regular investments. TIAA-CREF does not have a real estate fund as such, but a large portion of the investments of TIAA are in real estate and mortgages. TIAA-CREF also does not have a precious metals fund. Investors who want to have direct investments in real estate or precious metals should plan to include such holdings in their regular investment portfolio rather than in their retirement funds.

Bibliography

Brimelow, Peter, *The Wall Street Gurus,* Random House, 1986. A discussion of the best known writers and publishers who sell advice about the stock market.

Browne, Harry, and Coxen, Terry, *Inflation-Proofing Your Investments,* Morrow, 1981.

Bruck, Connie, *The Predator's Ball,* Simon and Schuster, 1988. An explanation of the development of high-risk, or "junk," bonds.

Casey, Douglas, *Strategic Investing,* Simon and Schuster, 1982.

Train, John, *The Money Masters,* Harper and Row, 1980. Brief biographical essays on the best known investment managers in recent years.

Selected Readings

General Financial Planning

Block, Stanley B., Peavy, John W. III, and Thornton, John, *Personal Financial Management,* Harper and Row, 1988.

Boone, Louis E., and Kurtz, David L., *Contemporary Personal Finance,* Random House, 1985.

Gitman, Lawrence J., and Joehnk, Michael D., *Personal Financial Planning,* Dryden Press, 1987.

Shane, Dorlene V., *Be Your Own Financial Planner,* John Wiley & Sons, 1987.

Skousen, Mark, *The Complete Guide to Financial Privacy,* Simon and Schuster, 1983.

Tobias, Andrew, *The Only Other Investment Guide You'll Ever Need,* Simon and Schuster, 1987.

Retirement and Estate Planning

Brosterman, Robert, *The Complete Estate Planning Guide,* New American Library, 1982.

Donoghue William E., *Investment Tips for Retirement Savings,* Harper and Row, 1987.

Grace, William E., *The ABCs of IRAs,* Dell, 1982.

Lochrey, Paul J. *The Financial Planner's Guide to Estate Planning,* Prentice-Hall, 1987.

Nichols, Donald R., *Life Cycle Investing,* Dow Jones-Irwin, 1985.

Vicker, Ray, *The Dow Jones-Irwin Guide to Retirement Planning,* Dow Jones-Irwin, 1987.

Investment Strategies—General

Browne, Harry, *The Economic Time Bomb,* St. Martin's Press, 1989.

Browne, Harry, *Why the Best-Laid Investment Plans Usually Go Wrong,* Morrow, 1987.

Donoghue, William E., with Tilling, Thomas, *Complete Money Market Guide,* Harper and Row, 1980.

Donoghue, William E., with Tilling, Thomas, *No-Load Mutual Fund Guide,* Harper and Row, 1981.

The Individual Investor's Guide to No-Load Mutual Funds, American Association of Individual Investors, 1989. This is an annual publication available from AAII.

Investment Strategies—Fundamental

Dreman, David, *The New Contrarian Investment Strategy,* Random House, 1982.

Graham, Benjamin, *The Intelligent Investor,* Harper and Row, 1973. This book, long considered the foundation of fundamental investing, went through four revisions. Another version, *Security Analysis,* co-authored with David L. Dodd and intended to be a college textbook, first appeared in 1934.

Loeb, Gerald M., *The Battle for Investment Survival,* Simon and Schuster, 1965. This book is also considered one of the classics of investment writing.

Lynch, Peter, *One Up on Wall Street,* Simon and Schuster, 1989.

Investment Strategies—Technical

Fosback, Norman G., *Stock Market Logic,* Institute for Econometric Research, 1981.

Merriman, Paul A., and Dowd, Merle, E., *Market Timing with No-Load Mutual Funds,* Henry Holt, 1986.

Pring, Martin, *Technical Analysis Explained,* McGraw-Hill, 1985.

Zweig, Martin, *Winning on Wall Street,* Warner Books, 1986. Zweig is considered an able technician, but his books include information on fundamental analysis as well.

Zweig, Martin, *Winning With New IRAs,* Warner Books, 1987.

Investments and Computers

Bookbinder, Albert I. A., *Computer-Assisted Investment Handbook,* Programmed Press, 1988.

Computerized Investing, American Association of Individual Investors, published bi-monthly.

Corney, William J., *Dynamic Stock Market Analysis with Dow Jones Market Analyzer PLUS,* Dow Jones-Irwin, 1986.

Meyers, Thomas A., *The Dow Jones-Irwin Guide to On-Line Investing,* Dow Jones-Irwin, 1987.

Woodwell, Donald, *Automating Your Financial Portfolio,* Dow Jones-Irwin, 1983.

Appendices

Appendix A

Selected TIAA-CREF Publications

- CREF Prospectus and Statement of Additional Information
- Transferring Accumulations in the TIAA-CREF System
- Supplemental Retirement Annuities
- CREF Stock and Money Market Units at Work
- Your TIAA-CREF Annuities and the TIAA Graded Benefit Payment Program
- TIAA-CREF Annual Report
- Rules for Determining Benefits
- Allocating Premiums in the TIAA-CREF System
- CREF Stock and Money Market Units at Work

The Personnel Office or Benefits Director at your institution may have copies of the publications listed in this appendix. If not, they can be obtained from TIAA-CREF by calling 1–800–842–2776, or by mail

Appendix B

TIAA-CREF Toll-free Numbers

Policyholder Information Center (1–800–842–2776)

Inquiries concerning annuity options, benefits, premiums, and accumulations.

Benefit Payment Information Center (1–800–842–2777)

Inquiries concerning benefit payments.

Allocation change and accumulation transfer (1–800–842–2252)

For making transfers, allocation changes, and finding accumulation balances.

CREF Accumulation Unit Values (1–800–223–1290)

For a 24 hour record message giving CREF accumulation unit values.

TIAA-CREF Publications (1–800–842–2733) Ext. 5509

To request publications

Tax Deferred Annuity Planning (1–800–223–1200)

Inquiries concerning TIAA-CREF SRA's and other optional retirement programs.

Tax Deferred Annuity Calculation Unit
 (1–800–842–2733) Ext. 2929

For a calculation of the maximum amount of salary that can be tax-deferred.

Appendix C

Some Independent Companies Offering Tax Sheltered Annuities

The Dreyfus Corporation
600 Madison Avenue
New York, NY 10022
1–800–645–6561

Fidelity Investments
82 Devonshire Street
Boston, MA 02109
1–800–544–6666

Investors Research Corporation
P.O. Box 200
Kansas City, MO 64141
1–800–345–2021

The Variable Annuity Life Insurance Company
390 Union Blvd. Suite 600
Lakewood, CO 80228
1–800–525–8453

T. Rowe Price Associates
100 E. Pratt St.
Baltimore, MD 21202
1–800–638–5660

Vanguard Group
Vanguard Financial Center
Valley Forge, PA 19482
1–800–662–7447

Appendix D

Investment Software Programs

General Financial Planning

Financial Navigator—Personal Version, MoneyCare Inc., 253 Martens Avenue, Suite 12, Mountain View, CA 94040. (800) 824–9827.

Managing Your Money, MECA Ventures, Inc., 355 Riverside Ave., Westport, CT 06880. (203) 226–2400.

MoneyCalc Premier, Money Tree Software, 1753 Wooded Knolls Drive, Suite 200, Philomath, OR 97370. (503) 929–2140.

Personal Financial Planner, TaxCalc Software, Inc., 4210 W. Vickery Blvd., Fort Worth, TX 76107. (817) 738–3122.

Plan Ahead, Advanced Financial Planning, 20922 Paseo Olma, El Toro, CA 92630. (714) 855–1578.

Portfolio Management

Market Manager Plus, Dow Jones & Co., P.O. Box 300, Princeton, NJ 08540. (800) 257–5144.

PC/Personal Investor, Best Programs, Inc., 2700 South Quincy Street, Arlington, VA 22206. (800) 368–2405.

Professional Portfolio—Level I, Advent Software, Inc., 512 Second Street, San Francisco, CA 94117.

Stock Manager, Analytical Service Associates, 21 Hollis Road, Lynn, MA 01904. (617) 593–2404.

Sylvia Porter's Personal Investment Manager, Timeworks, 444 Lake Cook Road, Deerfield, IL 60015. (800) 535–9497.

Fundamental Analysis

Economic Investor, ECON, One World Trade Center, Suite 7967, New York, NY 10048. (800) 628–2828, Ext. 799.

Fundamental Investor, Savant Corp., P.O. Box 440278, Houston, TX 77244. (800) 231–9900.

Market Microscope, Dow Jones & Co., P.O. Box 300, Princeton, NJ 08540. (800) 257–5114.

Stock Market Bargains, Dynacomp, Inc., 178 Phillips Road, Webster, NY 14580. (800) 828–6772.

Stockpak II, Standard & Poor's Corp., 25 Broadway, New York, NY 10004. (800) 852–5200.

Value/Screen Plus, Value Line Software, 711 Third Avenue, New York, NY 10017. (800) 654–0508.

Technical Analysis

Investment Analyst, Omni Software Systems, Inc., 146 N. Broad Street, Griffith, IN 46319. (219) 924–3522.

Market Analyzer Plus, Dow Jones & Co., P.O. Box 300, Princeton, NJ 08540. (800) 257–5114.

Stock Market Securities Program, 1015 Gayley Avenue, Suite 506, Los Angeles, CA 90024. (213) 476–4682.

Trendline II, Standard & Poor's Corp., 25 Broadway, New York, NY 10004. (800) 852–5200.

Wall Street Plotter, Dickens Data Systems, Inc., 6065 Atlantic Blvd., Suite A, Norcross, GA 30071. (404) 448–6177.

Real Estate Analysis

Mortgage Backed Securities Calculator, Bond-Tech, Inc., P.O. Box 192, Englewood, OH 45322. (513) 836–3991.

The Professional Real Estate Analyst, Coral Software, Inc., P.O. Box 18543, Seattle, WA 98118. (206) 723–4943.

Real Analyzer, Real-Comp, P.O. Box 1210, Cupertino, CA 95015. (408) 996–1160.

Real Estate Analysis Package, Execuware, Inc., 3640 Westgate Center Circle, Winston-Salem, NC 27103. (919) 760–3576.

Real Estate Model for the Eighties, Commercial Software Systems, Inc., 7689 W. Frost Drive, Littleton, CO 80123. (303) 973–1325.

Bond Analysis

Microcomputer Bond Program, Dynacomp, Inc., 178 Phillips Road, Webster, NY 14580. (800) 828–6772.

Bondpro, Techserve, Inc., P.O. Box 70056, Bellevue, WA 98007. (800) 826–8082.

Bondseye, Ergo, Inc., 1419 Wyant Road, Santa Barbara, CA 93108. (800) 772–6637.

Bondcalc, Personal Computer Products, 11200 Lockwood Drive, Suite 307, Silver Spring, MD 20901. (301) 593–2571.

MicroBond Calculator, Piedmont Software Co., 1130 Harding Place, Charlotte, NC 28204. (704) 376–0935.

Bonds and Interest Rates Software, Programmed Press, 599 Arnold Road, West Hempstead, NY 11552. (516) 599–6527.

Mutual Fund Analysis

Fund Profit, Guard Band, 138 N. Edinburg Ave., Los Angeles, CA 90048. (213) 931–4247.

Fundgraf, Parsons Software, 1230 W. 6th Street, Loveland, CO 80537. (303) 669–3744.

Mutual Fund Chartist, Strategic Timing, Inc., 534 S. Kansas Ave., #1440, Topeka, KS 66603. (913) 232–6226.

The Mutual Fund Investor, American River Software, 1523 Kingsford Drive, Carmichael, CA 95608. (916) 483–1600.

Mutual Gain, Bottom Line Solutions, 10125 Hermosa Way, La Mesa, CA 92041. (619) 447–7234.

Mutual Maid, John Nardy, 873 Little Bend Rd., Altamonte Springs, FL 32714. (305) 862–1390.

Tax Preparation

Aardvark 1040 Prep, CYMA/McGraw-Hill, 1400 E. Southern Avenue, Tempe, AZ 85283. (602) 831–2607.

EZTax-Plan, EZ Ware Corp., 29 Bala Avenue, Suite 206, Bala Cynwyd, PA 19004. (800) 543–1040.

MacIntax Federal, Software Inc., 4820 Adohr Lane, Suite F. Camarillo, CA 93010. (800) 622–6829. In spite of the name, this software is not limited to use on the MacIntosh.

Tax Preparer, HowardSoft, 1224 Prospect Street, Suite 150, La Jolla, CA 92037. (619) 454–0121.

Tax Pro, Cheaspeake Software, P.O. Box 1014, Richmond, VA 23208–1014. (804) 358–7802.

TurboTax Personal 1040, ChipSoft, Inc., 5045 Shoreham Place, Suite 100, San Diego, CA 92122. (619) 453–8722.

Free Software

The American Association of Individual Investors maintains an inventory of investment software available at no charge. Copies can be obtained from them for only a nominal charge for the disks and for mailing and handling. For information, contact American Association of Individual Investors, 625 N. Michigan Ave., Chicago, IL 60611. (312) 280–0170.

Appendix E

Useful Addresses

American Association of Individual Investors, 612 North Michigan, Chicago, IL 60611.

American Association of Retired Persons, 1909 K Street, NW, Washington, DC 20049.

Barrons, 200 Burnett Road, Chicopee, MA, 01021.

Business Week, 1221 Avenue of the Americas, New York, NY 10017.

Department of the Treasury, Bureau of the Public Debt, Washington, DC 20239. For information about U.S. Savings Bonds, Treasury Bills, Treasury Notes and Treasury Bonds.

Financial World, P.O. Box 10750, Des Moines, IA 50340.

Forbes, 60 5th Avenue, New York, NY 10011.

Fortune, 541 North Fairbanks Court, Chicago, IL 60611.

Money, Time-Life Building, Rockefeller Center, New York, NY 10020.

National Association of Investment Clubs, P.O. Box 220, Royal Oad, MI 48068.

National Council of Senior Citizens, 1511 K Street, NW, Washington, DC 20005.

National Council on Aging, 600 Maryland Avenue SW, Washington, DC 20024.

National Council on Teacher Retirement, 275 Broad Street, Columbus, OH 43215.

National Retired Teachers Association, 1909 K Street NW, Washington, DC 20036.

No-Load Portfolios, 527 Hotel Plaza, Boulder City, NV 89005.

Pension Benefit Guarantee Corporation, Suite 700, 2020 K Street, Washington, DC 20006.

Standard and Poor's Outlook, 25 Broadway, New York, NY 10004.

Teachers Insurance and Annuity Association—College Retirement Equities Fund (TIAA-CREF), 730 Third Avenue, New York, NY 10017.

Value Line, 711 Third Avenue, New York, NY 10017.

Wall Street Journal, 22 Cortlandt Street, New York, NY 10007.

Request For Additional Information

The following information is available at no charge for readers of this book. Mail to: No-Load Portfolios, 527 Hotel Plaza, Boulder City, Nevada 89005.

☐ I would like to be placed on your mailing list to receive occasional updates concerning new TIAA-CREF offerings.

☐ I would like a free copy of the *No-Load Portfolios* Newsletter.

☐ I would like a free copy of Paul Merriman's *Fund Exchange* Newsletter, and a free audio-tape entitled, "Understanding Market Timing."

Name: _____

Address: _____

_____

_____

Order Form For Additional Books

Kendall/Hunt Publishing Company
2460 Kerper Boulevard
Dubuque, Iowa 52001
319–588–1451

I wish to order *Managing Your TIAA-CREF Retirement Accounts.*

_____ Copies at $19.95, total: _____

Shipping and Handling ($2.00 ea.) _____

Grand Total: _____

Name: _____

Address: _____

_____

_____

_____

Discounts are available for quantities exceeding ten books. Call Kendall/Hunt Publishing at 319–588–1451 for details.

About the Authors . . .

DR. LEONARD E. GOODALL is Professor of Management and Public Administration at the University of Nevada, Las Vegas. He is also former President of that institution and former Chancellor of the University of Michigan-Dearborn. He is a graduate of Central Missouri State University, has a master's degree from the University of Missouri and a Ph.D. in political science and economics from the University of Illinois. He is a Certified Financial Planner.

DR. WILLIAM J. CORNEY is Professor of Management at the University of Nevada, Las Vegas. He has an electrical engineering degree from the University of Michigan-Dearborn, a Master of Business Administration degree from Eastern Michigan University, and a Ph.D. from Arizona State University. He is a Certified Internal Auditor and is author of *Dynamic Stock Market Analysis,* published by Dow Jones-Irwin.

Both authors are frequent lecturers at seminars and institutes on investments and financial planning, and they are co-editors of NO-LOAD PORTFOLIOS, a monthly newsletter concerning investments and no-load mutual funds.

Index

AARP General Bond Fund, 122
Accumulations, 29–30
Advance-Decline line, 60–64
 calculations for, 63
Allocations, 47
Annual annuity benefits report, 93, 94
Annuity income, 100–106
 one-life options, 101–102
 questions to ask, 105
 phasing-in, 104
 survivor options, 102–103
 TIAA payment methods, 103–104
Asset Allocations, 29–39, 45–46
Automated Telephone Service, 93, 95–98
 accumulation transfers, 96
 allocation changes, 97
 current annuity value, 95
 multiple transactions, 98

Barrons, 62, 69, 83, 115
Blue Chip Value Fund, 120
Bonds, 7, 120–130, 143
 municipal, 121–122
 value changes, 83
Bond mutual funds, 122–123
Browne, Harry, 30–31, 127
Bull and Bear Gold Investors Fund, 129
Bull and Bear magazine, 69
Bull and Bear U.S. Government Securities Fund, 122
Business cycle, 77–82
Buy and hold strategy, 49

C-curve, 87–88
Capital Preservation Treasury Note Trust fund, 122
Cash and cash equivalents, 7, 112, 123
Cash payments form TIAA-CREF, 99
Certificates of Deposit, 123
Closed end mutual funds, 118, 120
Colby, Robert W., 64, 66
Common stocks, 113–120
 price to earnings ratios, 114–116
 yield, 114–115
Computerized financial software, 68–69, 142–145

Computers, 136–137, 142–145
Consistency, 51
Corney, William J., 74, 149
CREF Actively Managed Equities fund, 14, 19, 24–27, 31, 32, 34, 36, 42
CREF Balanced fund, 14, 19, 26, 33, 86–89
CREF Bond fund, 14, 19, 24, 26, 31–34, 82–86, 88, 111, 122
CREF Group Retirement Annuity II, 99
CREF International fund, 14, 19, 26, 32, 34, 42, 89–90, 118
CREF Passive Equities fund, 14, 19, 24, 26, 33, 90–91
CREF Stock fund, 12, 15, 30, 42, 52, 54, 59, 62, 88, 111
 composition, 60
 performance, 60
CREF Money Market fund, 14, 24–25, 31, 32, 34, 36–38, 43, 52, 54, 59, 83, 111, 124

Defined contribution plan, 15
Defined income plan, 15
Diversification, 6–7, 51, 118
Dollar averaging strategies, 41–46
 philosophy of, 42
Donoghue, William, 35–36
Dow Jones Market Analyzer PLUS, 68
Dreyfus A Bonds Plus fund, 122
Dreyfus Fund, 119
Dreyfus Tax Exempt, 123

Emergency funds, 5, 124
Equities, 7, 113–123
Evergreen Global Real Estate Equity fund, 127

Federal Reserve, 55, 78
 and stock market performance, 56
Fidelity Magellan fund, 117, 119
Fidelity Precious Metals and Minerals fund, 129
Fidelity Short Term Tax Free Bond fund, 123
Fidelity Strategic Gold fund, 129
Fifty percent solution, 110
Financial Dynamics fund, 119
Financial inventory, 2
Financial planning, 1–9, 135, 142

Financial Select Income fund, 122
Financial U.S. Government Bond fund, 122
Financial World, 69
Fundamental Analysis, 114–116, 136, 142
Fund Exchange newsletter, 70
    timing model results, 71

General Electric, 113, 120–121
General Motors Corporation, 113
Gemini II Capital fund, 120
Gold, 30–31, 127–129
    bullion, 128
    coins, 128
Goodall, Leonard E., 149
Graded benefit method, 94, 103–104

Hirsch, Yale, 67
Hunt brothers, 129

IBM, 113
Interest Payment Retirement Option (IPRO), 100
Interest Rates, 53
    as a warning flag, 53
    effect on investments, 49
    indicators, 55
Interest Rate Review newsletter, 85
Investment pyramid, 6, 7
Investment Strategy, 5, 19–28, 135–136
Investor's Daily newspaper, 59, 64, 65, 69
    psychological market indicators, 65
Individual Retirement Account (IRA), 99, 119
    American eagle coins in, 128
Inflation, effects on, 130

"Junk" bonds, 121

Korea fund, 120

Level benefit method, 94, 103–104
Leverage, 125
Load mutual funds, 118
Long range goals, 3
Lynch Peter, 117

Market Logic newsletter, 69
Merriman, Paul, 70, 71
Meyers, Thomas A., 64, 66
Money market funds, 123–124
Monthly allocations, 29–30
Mutual funds, 118–128, 144
    open-end, 118
    closed-end, 118
    load, 118
    no-load, 119

National Association of College and University Business Officers, 13
Net worth, statement of, 4
New York Stock Exchange, 113–115, 119
No-load mutual funds, 119
No-Load Portfolios newsletter, 70, 84
    bond timing model, 84
Non-TIAA-CREF retirement plans, 17
    timing indicators, 72
Nurock, Robert, 64

Obtaining retirement benefits, 98–106
Open-end mutual funds, 118

Palladium, 128
PepsiCo, 114–115
Permanent allocation strategies, 30–34
    age related allocation strategy, 34
    equal allocation strategy, 30–33
    investor selected allocation strategy, 33–34
Personal financial planning, 2, 109–110
Personal identification number (PIN), 95
Platinum, 128
Precious metals, 7, 127, 129
    bullion certificates, 128
    mutual funds, 128–129
Price, T. Rowe, Realty Income Fund, 127
Price, T. Row, Tax Free Income fund, 123
Prime rate, 84
Pring, Martin, 85, 87
Procter and Gamble, 113
Publications (selected) of TIAA-CREF, 139

Quarterly Confirmation of Transactions report, 97
Quarterly statements, 93–94

Real estate, 7, 112, 125–127, 143
    tax benefits, 126
    investment trusts, 126
    limited partnerships, 126
    mutual funds, 126
Retirement income, 15–16, 130–131
    monthly withdrawals for, 131
Retirement planning, 8–9, 129–132, 135
Risk tolerance, 22
Rukeyeser, Louis, 64

Safeco municipal bond fund, 123
S & P 500, 59–60
    as an indicator, 59
Scudder Income fund, 122
Selected readings, 135–137
    general financial planning, 135
    investment strategies—fundamental, 136
    investment strategies—general, 135

investment strategies—technical, 136
investments and computers, 136
retirement and estate planning, 135
Services of TIAA-CREF, 93–108
Silver, 128–129
Social Security, 130–133
Source Capital fund, 120
Stock price trends, 54
as a warning flag, 54
Stoken, Richard, 67
Stoken Strategic Climate model, 67
Strong Municipal Bond fund, 123
Strong Short Term Bond fund, 122
Supplemental Retirement Annuities (SRA's), 16–17, 106–107, 119
Systems and Forecasts newsletter, 70
momentum oscillator, 75
monetary filter, 75
time trend III results, 73

Tax preparation, 144
Tax sheltered annuities (TSA's), 106–107, 119, 141
independent companies offering, 141
Technical analysis, 114, 116–118, 136, 143
Telephone numbers (TIAA-CREF), 140
Ten percent solution, 109, 110
The Participant newsletter, 99
TIAA-CREF, 11–14, 139–140
criticisms of, 13
history, 11–12
new fund options, 14
phone numbers, 140
publications, 139
TIAA fund, 11, 12, 14, 15, 19, 22, 26, 27, 30, 32, 33, 34, 111, 112, 127
Timer Digest newsletter, 70

timing signals, 76
Tokyo stock exchange, 115
Transferring funds, 47–76
incremental transfers, 52
economic evidence approach, 52–59
minimums, 48
principles for, 50–52
reasons for transferring, 48–50
when posting occurs, 48
Treasury bills, 123–124
Twentieth Century Select fund, 119
Twentieth Century U.S. Government Bond fund, 122

Unisex mortality tables, 100, 105–106
Unit value, 94
Useful addresses, 146
U.S. Gold Trust fund, 129
U.S. Real Estate fund, 127

Value Line Investment Survey, 116
Vanguard Gold and Precious Metals fund, 129
Vanguard U.S. Treasury Bond fund, 122
Variable allocation strategies, 34–38
interest rate strategy, 35–36
trend reversal strategy, 37–38
Veilleux, E.D., 63

Wall Street Journal, 66
Wall Street Week Elves indicator, 64

Yield curve, 56–58
inverted yield curve, 56, 57
normal yield curve, 57

Zweig fund, 120
Zweig, Martin, 37–38, 66, 85